TO MY FAMILY

TORRE REFORMA

L. BENJAMÍN ROMANO

TEXTS

ALI MALKAWI
FRANCISCO SERRANO
FELIPE LEAL
L. BENJAMÍN ROMANO

PHOTOGRAPHY

IWAN BAAN
ALFONSO MERCHAND

Arquine

TORRE REFORMA
L. Benjamín Romano

First edition, 2019
© Arquine, S.A. de C.V.
Amsterdam 163 A, Hipódromo,
Mexico City, 06100
ISBN: 978-607-9489-43-4

TEXTS
© Ali Malkawi
© Felipe Leal
© Francisco Serrano
© L. Benjamín Romano
© Miquel Adrià

PHOTOGRAPHS
© Iwan Baan
© Alfonso Merchand

Arquine

DIRECTOR
Miquel Adrià

CHIEF EDITOR
Selene Patlán

EDITORIAL ASSISTANTS
Brenda Soto, Miguel Caballero

LBR arquitectos

PUBLISHING COORDINATORS
Lilian Levy, Zuany Díaz

PLANS
LBR arquitectos
University of Pennsylvania

DESIGN
Gabriela Varela + David Kimura

COPY EDITING
Beatriz Stellino

PREPRESS
Emilio Breton

ENGLISH TRANSLATIONS AND COPY EDITING
Fionn Petch
Quentin Pope

www.arquine.com

This book was made possible thanks to the support of:

CEMEX
Construyendo un mejor futuro

Grupo HeG

GRUPO tecno
Soluciones en Vidrio y Aluminio

GRUPO ARCA
MARMOLES ARCA · PRATO XX · THE WOODSHOP

Schindler

CONTENTS

FOREWORD

ALI MALKAWI

Situated in the heart of Mexico City, Torre Reforma heralds a new era in design for the city. The construction's form and aesthetic reflect a rising concern for building performance, both environmentally and functionally.

The basic philosophy of minimal environmental impact has been deployed in this structure. The building successfully connects to its urban context with the lowest or most positive effect on its surroundings while also creating a healthy indoor environment.

Environmental principles were applied with predictive techniques early in the design process to enhance their applicability, and to promote an integrated design. The result is a building in which performance is enhanced and has become a core element of the design.

Benjamin Romano and I met for the first time a few years ago in New York City, to discuss the performance intention of this building. At that time, we identified the two core drivers in energy-efficient design for tall buildings that we might consider: natural ventilation and solar access. Benjamin had already studied many complex elements affecting the building. He was seeking simulation studies to inform and inspire innovations in building performance design closely connected to the microclimate of the site. This simulation work, in concert with analyses of other aspects of the building by other consultants, provided crucial information used in the design and development of Torre Reforma's concept.

The building's orientation on its site optimizes views from the interior while shielding the building from the sun in summer, and heating the building during the winter. Openings in the façade take advantage of the prevailing winds for ventilation, thus lessening the building's reliance on mechanical fans and directly connecting the building with the outside environment.

Torre Reforma offers an alternative to the familiar all-glass, tall commercial buildings that have, in many instances, little to do with their context, culture or environment. The architecture of Torre Reforma is true to the concept of integration in many ways: structure, function, environment, and aesthetics have all been carefully orchestrated to create a dynamic and functional high-rise sculpture that respects its context and surroundings.

The experience a building offers combined with the quality of its spaces and durability of its function are fundamental to its evaluation. Torre Reforma succeeds on several fronts, providing unique efficiencies and experiences throughout. Beyond quantifiable efficiencies—including the effective use of energy, water, and financial resources—the building's spaces are also well-conceived. Innovative solutions include breathable triple-height patios and gardens, as well as lighting and thermal solutions that provide visual interest and sensory variations throughout. Offering occupants this variety of spaces and experiences adds an intrinsic value to the building's sustainability.

As a result, this work of architecture is not only environmentally responsive but also uniquely connected to place, seamlessly weaving a new Mexican style with the functional requirements of a modern office building. Torre Reforma introduces an architectural aesthetic that enriches the urban landscape while acting as an example of a well-balanced and efficient high-rise in its design, construction and operation.

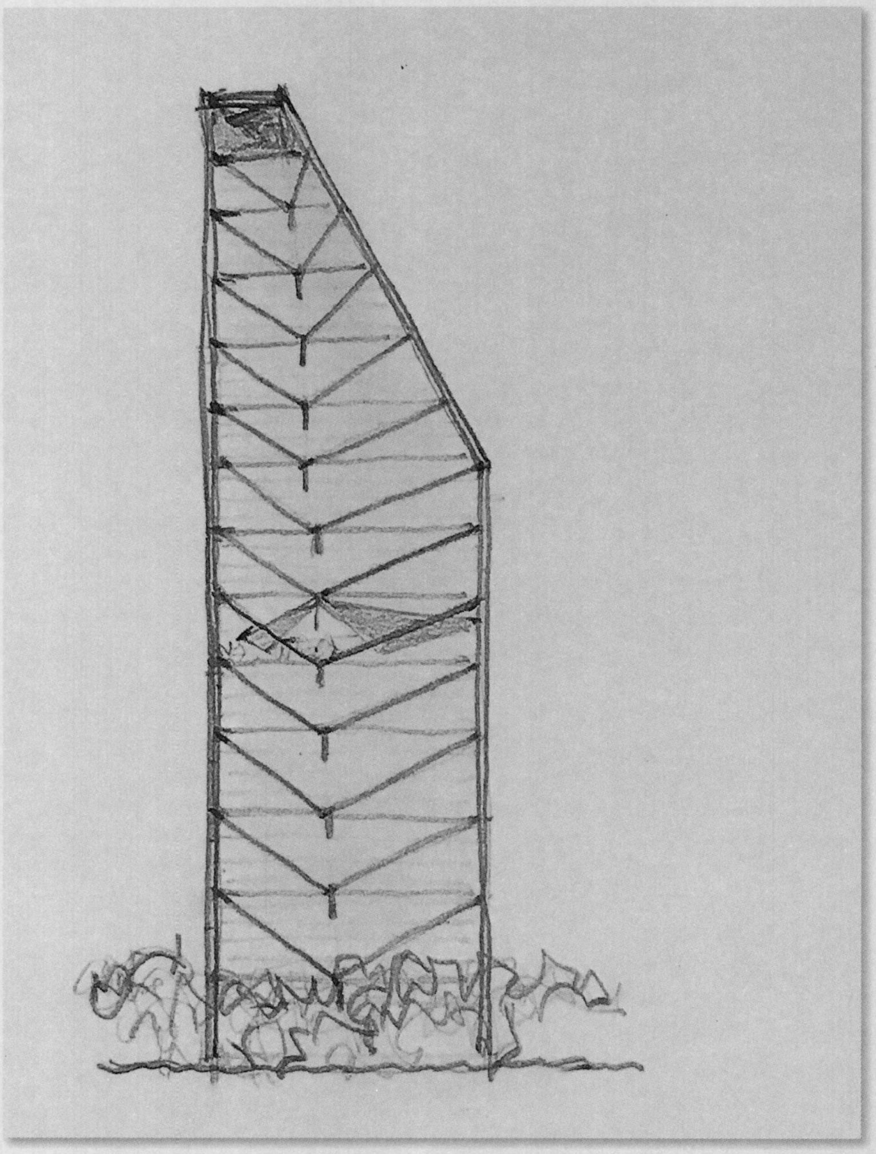

PRESENTATION

FRANCISCO SERRANO

Many people can talk about Torre Reforma, but to me the most interesting thing about my friend and colleague Benjamín is his roundedness as a human being. Architects often only design or only plan, build or promote projects, whereas Benjamín's life is far more complete: he promotes, plans, delivers and sells. He offers the whole package, and that is what makes him exceptional. His architecture is connected to society, without merely obeying financial considerations; it contributes something to the city. He is well-educated in every sense of the world.

Certain milestones in Benjamín's career as an architect marked changes that have led him to express himself differently. Torre Chapultepec is one example of his outstanding achievements, along with other projects of great significance that many people unfamiliar with his work don't understand how to read. Torre Tres Picos and the Centro de Cómputo de Tizayuca speak volumes. His work is all-encompassing, merging form, function and financial considerations into a single whole.

Furthermore, few architects are good teachers and able to engage in broad-ranging discussions. Unlike the engineer who merely spouts out tedious calculations, or the architect who teaches composition to his or her students but doesn't care how a design can actually be built, Benjamín has succeeded in communicating a more holistic approach. That is why, a few years ago, when we finally managed to bring the Cátedra Blanca university course from Spain to Mexico, I immediately thought of him as the right person to deliver it.

This academic experience formed the basis of a friendship that I cannot disassociate from discussing his work. As frequent traveling companions, Benjamín and I have discovered architecture from around the world, and all of these experiences have shown me his character: he is always himself, his interest never waivers and he becomes animated by a good work of architecture. He is also just as stubborn as I am, and when our views differ he becomes cross, and he tries to set me straight. On our journeys we have sometimes met world-renowned architects and seen their works; they have to some extent educated us, because we have sought out these experiences instead of being chance encounters. Not every architect is willing or able to travel the world to expand their knowledge, have conversations, and see things for themselves.

Journeys are the best way of meeting people, and they also give architects a chance to discover true inspiration. Yes, Benjamín may become visibly excited when he sees a work of architecture, but he is not simply impressed by scale or an unusual structure. He takes in everything and then discusses its strengths and weaknesses. His views are objective and well-grounded. We have seen various buildings under construction, including works by Rudy Ricciotti, Zaha Hadid and Jean Nouvel, and Benjamín has a unique perspective on them, by focusing on what construction companies do well or badly, and even their rental potential. He's interested in the process, where the only way of arriving at a form is not based on a mock-up.

At a restaurant in Zurich, he once told me: "I'm going to show you my ideas for a building on Paseo de la Reforma." Then he drew the tower on a napkin and asked my opinion. He explained to me the process (at that time he did not mention the book) and said he was planning a triangle positioned at a right angle in order for the pre-existing house to remain in the center—a structurally viable proposition. I mention this because Benjamín shares his ideas so that you can support or criticize him; he isn't trying to boost his ego or brag about his work, and this is the attitude of a good architect. In this case, it was a sign of friendship, but ultimately he was looking for the way to do his best within his capabilities, a rare quality among architects.

For Torre Reforma, he bought a plot of land in partnership with his siblings, and together they chose the best site for the skyscraper. Then he decided against what most other architects would have done: simply demolish the old mansion in order to erect his new structure. Instead, Benjamín analyzed the possibilities and chose to preserve the pre-existing construction, not only as a unique structural challenge due to the required cuts in the foundations and its temporary relocation, and so on, but also so that the city could retain a small memento of Paseo de la Reforma's former appearance. In my view, the house is not an exceptional work of architecture, but it is generally representative of the houses that lined the avenue and is therefore a significant cultural legacy for the capital.

I was privy to the tower's many interesting details because Benjamín invited me to accompany him from the time he made his first sketch all the way to a meeting with

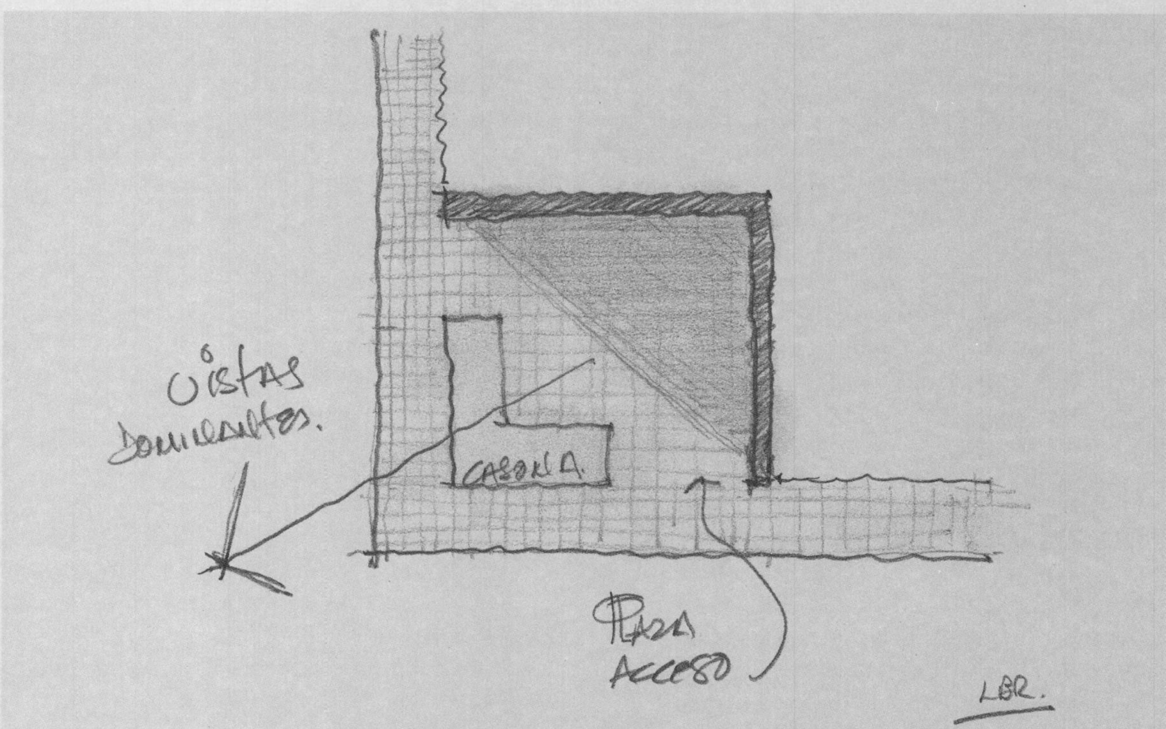

Arup in New York. I realized then that Benjamín would not be overawed by the firm's prestige, nor would he simply follow orders blindly. He sought the best people to see the project through and to work out the details together, that's all. I remember clearly that during the meeting a disagreement about the windows arose, and we left the room dissatisfied with Arup's proposal. On a similar occasion, when I took part in a competition with Norman Foster—which we ended up losing—I remember having a similar discussion, until Foster said: "What Serrano is suggesting is far more logical than what we've been talking about." I mention this because often you do not express your views—you think you're talking to a genius and so you accept everything they say despite your misgivings. Benjamín wasn't intimidated, though he was concerned about the investment. Therefore, once equipped with the calculations for the entire building, he asked for a second opinion from a structural expert from WSP, someone I had met during the project with Foster. Benjamín was looking for the best in terms of the process and everything else; he wanted to be on solid ground; he was not motivated by arrogance.

I followed the construction process too, and saw how Benjamín's interest was focused on producing the best possible work of architecture, and also the most economical, in the good sense of the word. Not the cheapest but the most effective. He also insisted on the quality of the architectural details, and this is clearly visible in the structure. We discussed the entire process, a couple of times even with the engineers. Benjamín wanted to give the structure an elegant skin, like Foster's Hearst Tower in New York, but I dissuaded him: the expression of the tower's outer envelope is clearly readable, regardless of the underlying technical justifications, as it gives meaning to the entire building, but this would be unnecessary for Torre Reforma. In the end he accepted my point of view.

The lack of columns is a distinguishing feature of Torre Reforma. It's a unique feat, creating open-plan spaces of

700 to 1,000 m², supported by a structure that expresses its form: it is not hidden, and it has a large and obvious span. There are also the clusters, unlike any other building in Mexico. Every few levels, a shared space has been left to allow for offices' potential growth. The only similar precedent in Mexico is Augusto H. Álvarez's La Mitra, which includes a patio every few floors. This idea is interesting because it refers to a characteristic of modern society: flexibility. Architects cannot expand buildings ad infinitum, and an alternative is to connect three levels at one point and with a staircase you allow users to climb up or down a level, doubling the surface area. There are also the famous atria without a single pane of glass: the best urban terrace in the city. Benjamín proposed this idea in his studio, and everyone feared that it would sacrifice the façade's flow. When he asked my opinion. I told him: "go ahead and open it up, you're the boss."

The building's warped metal framing, achieved through the use of 1.05 × 2.10 m modules, a dimension chosen due to the manufacturer's specifications, which can produce this size of panel and keep them in stock in case of a broken window or as required. This is indicative of Benjamín's approach; he doesn't just complete projects but also shows concern about their future lifespan, operation, and maintenance. I'd also like to mention the treatment given to the façade, which protects against insolation and increases the structure's aesthetic appeal. Architects rarely do something like that due to the money required. But Benjamín, apart from being an architect, is also the owner of the firm together with his siblings, and in this case commercial interests yielded to architectural considerations.

Torre Reforma's robotic parking facility is another outstanding feature: this structure is designed to be convertible into something else if the world changes and fewer parking spaces are required in the future. Benjamín was seen as a visionary when he planned it, but now this formula appears to be an obligatory requirement. He also made a positive change to the Temporary Revocable Permit to alter the traffic direction in this section; cars can now access Río Elba street from both directions, preventing traffic build-up on Atoyac street.

This project is not just another building or box with attached ornamentation or gratuitous deformations. Its form is unique due to the plot and the design of its parking facility. Torre Reforma will never be mistaken for the tower next door, but at the same time it flatters the neighboring constructions as part of an improved context.

A good building begins with a good parti, and in this case, it began with a napkin: it was all there from the very beginning. Benjamín said: "on this site, I'm going to make this shape, and place it in this way in order to give views onto Chapultepec Park, with apertures on this side because I have an adjacency, with a setback from the narrow street and then on the main avenue I'll make a twist in order to reduce its impact." That's the parti. It was all there on the napkin and then it evolved. But the napkin on its own was enough to express the parti, because the design had effectively already been resolved by the architect. Benjamín is a complete architect with a unique character, and hopefully Torre Reforma will herald more such exemplary projects.

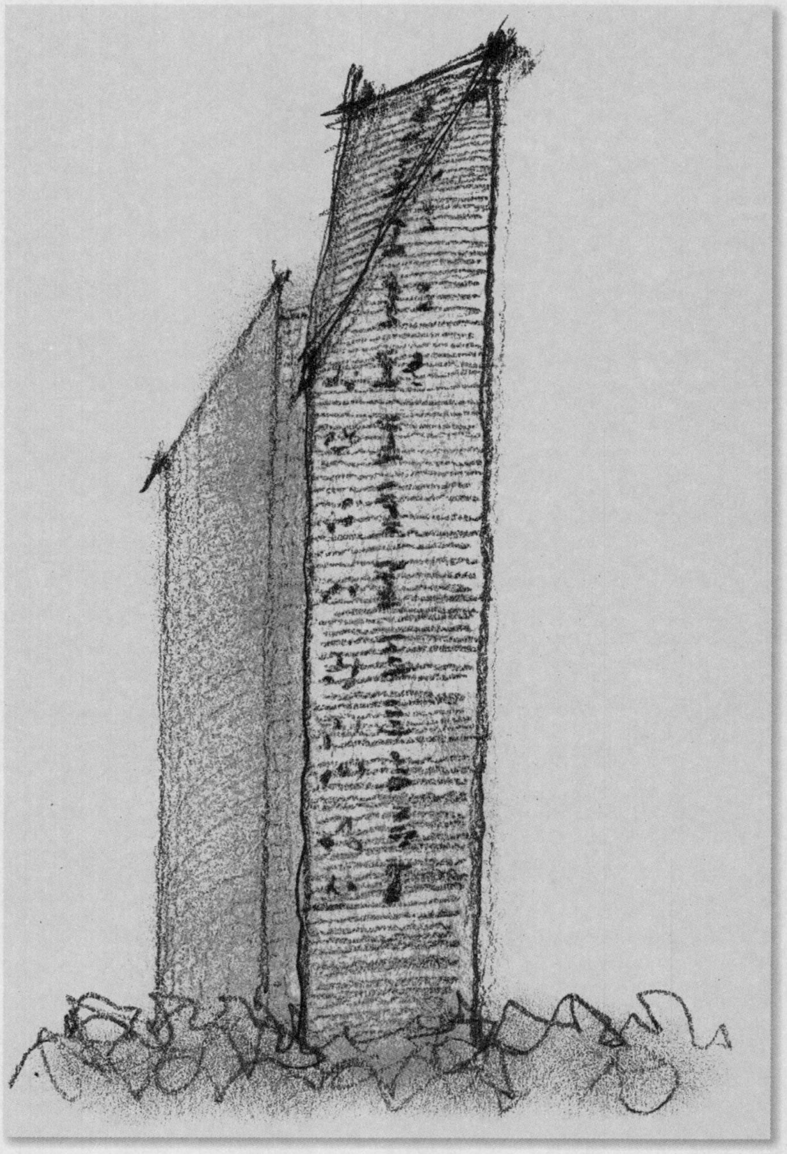

THE RENOVATION OF PASEO DE LA REFORMA, 2000–2004

FELIPE LEAL

Gaps and empty spaces began to open up in parts of central Mexico City during the 1990s. The capital's urban and social structures had suffered badly in the preceding decade; the Historic Center and central districts were the worst affected by the ravages of the 1985 earthquakes. As a result, new office, residential and commercial buildings needed by the city initially shifted westward, towards the fast-developing Santa Fe and the higher and lower parts of the upscale neighborhood of Lomas de Chapultepec; they also moved south, along the city's main north-south axis of Insurgentes Sur and flanking the Periferico beltway in the Ajusco area.

In the last decade of the twentieth century, the city center was dotted with empty lots. After the demolition or collapse of the pre-existing constructions, these properties ended up virtually frozen due to the lack of investment and depopulation in the damaged areas. Once-elegant avenues and neighborhoods such as Tabacalera, Doctores, Juárez, San Rafael, and Santa María La Ribera that were lined with iconic buildings were steadily falling into neglect; some of these areas were connected by the Paseo de la Reforma, undoubtedly the most important avenue both for the city and the country.

This stretch of road—formerly known as Paseo de la Emperatriz, a route laid out by Maximilian of Habsburg, Emperor of Mexico, to connect Chapultepec Castle to the Alameda and National Palace—resonated with symbolism during the twentieth century thanks to the construction of a series of *glorietas* or traffic circles: the Column of Independence and monuments built in honor of Cuauhtémoc, Colón and Bolívar; the equestrian sculpture of Charles IV, commonly known as El Caballito, which once stood at the intersection with Avenida Juárez and is now located opposite the National Art Museum (Munal); Diana the Huntress, a fountain incorporating a beautiful sculpture of the mythological figure. This statue departed from a purely symbolic representation, scandalizing conservative and closed-minded critics because of the voluptuousness of the nude figure. Mansions and stately houses dating from the Porfirio Díaz era stood proudly all along Paseo de la Reforma and were joined some decades later by Carlos Obregón Santacilia's health ministry and social security institute buildings; subsequently, the Hotel Reforma and modern office blocks were erected around the Glorieta de Colón. At this location and on adjacent corners, Augusto H. Álvarez, Mario Pani, Juan Sordo Madaleno and José Villagrán produced works that came to define Mexico City's urban appearance of the 1950s and 1960s. This image, combined with Pani's innovative condominiums, became an icon of a modern, cosmopolitan metropolis replete with spaces for recreational pursuits and a thriving nightlife. Restaurants, bars, movie theaters, cabarets, party halls and cafés shared the same area as the new hotels, financial centers, diplomatic representations and travel agencies.

A few years previously, in around 1945 or 1946, the tirelessly inventive Mario Pani decided that the city's new heart, corresponding to the "Mexican miracle," needed to be placed at the intersection of Paseo de la Reforma with Avenida de los Insurgentes, seeing this location as an essential geographical reference point for the city's layout, and a springboard for a flagship project of the city's various new downtown areas. His plan was to create a wide-open plaza, shaped like a *glorieta*, with the Monument to Cuauhtémoc in the middle; the Avenida de los Insurgentes would be routed underneath it through a tunnel, and a number of office buildings, residential constructions, hotels, restaurants and cafés would make this area a bustling public hub for the city. In the event, the only part of this project to be executed was the moving of the Monument to Cuauhtémoc to the intersection between Reforma and Insurgentes and the construction of the former Hotel Plaza, its concave façade suggesting the analogous compositional plan for the entire complex. The project was so bold that several of Pani's critics pressured neighbors and politicians to prevent it from going ahead, orchestrating a campaign with the slogan: "Si es de Pani, es de Pánico," which could be roughly translated as "If it's by Pani, it's time to Panic."

This background is important because it shows how Paseo de la Reforma was already being touted in those years as the ideal location for high-rise, mixed-use buildings that could constitute new urban thoroughfares to cope with the city's steady growth and diversification. Below I will outline what I see developing now at the intersection between Lieja and Ródano, at the edge of Chapultepec Park, at the entrance or gateway to Paseo de la Reforma, which has gradually become a new central location.

THE RENOVATION OF PASEO DE LA REFORMA, 2000-2004

However, this is not a Pani-style integral project conceived by a single architect; this time around, the development is following a different process and has other characteristics.

By the late twentieth century, the Paseo de la Reforma was in a sorry state, lined by several pieces of vacant land—small plots previously occupied by modest-sized, low-rise buildings, as well as some derelict single-family residences. Most of the grand buildings were dilapidated and had fallen into disuse. The movie theaters that lit up the area in the 1950s and 60s had begun retreating due to the onward march of television and the subsequent advent of the VCR; their doors were closed and they awaited a new breath of life or faced definitive closure. Notable examples include Cine Chapultepec—where the Torre Mayor now stands—and the Paseo, París, Roble and Latino movie theatres. The Cine Diana is the only one still standing, albeit with several of its screens now vandalized. Airline offices and ticketing outlets, as well as tourism agencies and financial headquarters, had all gradually moved westwards to other parts of the city such as Polanco, Lomas, and Santa Fe, as well as to the south. Housing for middle-income families, with the exception of Pani's condominiums at the intersection of the Varsovia and Guadalquivir streets, had virtually disappeared. The effects of this phenomenon were similar to the Historic Center in previous years: depopulation, a dwindling nightlife, a lack of building maintenance and public spaces, failing services, plummeting tourism numbers, and the closure of offices, stores and restaurants, as businesses left the area for other parts of the city.

To compound the lack of new buildings and new uses, public spaces and pedestrianized areas such as sidewalks, walkways, central reservations, green spaces, benches and street furniture, were all in a poor state of repair. The last intervention on the Paseo de la Reforma had taken place in 1968 in preparation for the Summer Olympics: clay paving stones had been laid along the sidewalks and some decorative features added. In the year 2000, at the turn of the century and 32 years after the last work, this paving was no longer fit for purpose. The clay was slippery, particularly during the rainy season; cracks had appeared all along the avenue which was littered with a chaotic array of manhole covers for electrical installations, drainage pipes and telephone cables, lacking the proper conduits and trenches. It looked more like the flooring of someone's home patio than a surface suitable for the urban scale and dimensions of the avenue. The street lights shone onto the roads, for the benefit of cars and buses, but lighting for the pedestrian sections was poor and badly distributed. The planters and green borders were defined by hedges that joined a series of discontinuous walkways, the result of repeated improvisations. Despite the ample areas of central reservations and walkways, little consideration was given to pedestrians.

The street furniture was characterless and poorly designed; the newspaper kiosks, shoeshine chairs and any number of rickety metal street stalls encroached upon street corners, creating obstacles for the natural routes taken by pedestrians and constituting visual barriers. This affected every sidewalk. Nor was there a single zebra crossing worthy of the name at any of the major junctions. Along the sidewalks the monuments and their plinths, as well as the sculptures of famous figures of the Reform period, all showed signs of deterioration and lacked lighting.

Given this desolate panorama and the large urban void spreading unchecked throughout the city center at the dawn of the new century, a radical intervention was required to return this area to its original role, to provide the necessary structure and support to improve Mexico City's urban image and help it regain its rightful stature.

In view of this situation, in the year 2000 the Mexico City government—through its tourism department—invited the Architecture Faculty of the National Autonomous University of Mexico (UNAM) to draw up the masterplan for the "Corredor Turístico Cultural Paseo de la Reforma." This infrastructure development program was coordinated by the writer Julieta Campos, then working as Mexico City's Tourism Minister, and by myself, Felipe Leal, in my capacity as Director of the UNAM's Faculty of Architecture at the time.

We set up an interdisciplinary team consisting of faculty members who were architects, engineers, urban designers, landscape artists, industrial designers and students at the UNAM. We began our work in 2000 and completed the project, in parallel with some works and other initiatives, in 2004. We divided the work into two phases. We started by drawing up an overall diagnosis and defining the strategies, detailed analyses and an executive project for the paving materials, street furniture, street lighting, signposting and vegetation. We designed benches, light posts, hedges, manhole covers, drains, pedestrian crossings, signage and traffic light posts.

In the second phase, in order to increase the number of visitors and tours along the Paseo de la Reforma, a concession was negotiated with a transport company to create the Turibús, a service that initially ran between the National Auditorium and the city's Zócalo or central square. We also set up a tourist police force to assist visitors and a contract was signed with a maintenance provider to keep the pavements, benches, vegetation and lighting in good condition and to implement a rolling street-cleaning program. Bus bays were added along the stretch of Reforma running alongside Chapultepec Park, and these included services such as public toilets and cafeterias. One of them now even includes a bookstore and other services for visitors.

Perhaps the most important physical intervention, apart from the new paving and vegetation planted all along the avenue, was at the intersection of Reforma with Insurgentes, a hub for the city's two most important thoroughfares, and formerly "kilometer zero" for the country's railway and highway infrastructure. We brought the Monument to Cuauhtémoc back to its original location at this junction after completely renovating its pyramid-shaped plinth, sculpture and the pointed-arch plaza surrounding the monument. As mentioned above, it had been moved during the 1940s as part of Mario Pani's urban project, but it did not work visually and also obstructed the route of the Metrobús (rapid bus transit) along Insurgentes, aside from the fact that it did not correspond to the *glorieta*'s original layout.

An essential part of the masterplan was to recommend new zoning regulations for the Borough of Cuauhtémoc. This paved the way for the borough administration to enable the merging of small plots to encourage verticalization through the construction of taller buildings, taking into account the breadth of the sections along Paseo de la Reforma. Tax incentives were also introduced to stimulate local real-estate development; those investing in Paseo de la Reforma were granted tax relief for up to a decade, and fast-track systems helped to cut red tape and make it more straightforward to apply for permits. The Torre Mayor was the only construction of this type in existence at that time, and a sign of things to come; though it appeared isolated and without a proper context, it already pointed to the start of a much-needed recovery.

The city's investment proved successful in improving its public space in order to restore the dignity to this central location and to encourage investment after 2004, the project's completion date. At least 15 projects for building complexes or high-rise towers have emerged, bringing back hotels, shopping malls, movie theaters, mid-level and luxury residential housing developments, offices for Mexico's leading financial institutions, along with a wide range of services.

The Torre Reforma, an extraordinary work of architecture and undoubtedly the most compelling construction along the avenue today, is the outcome of this integrative process described above. The tower is innovative for several reasons: it imaginatively takes advantage of the lower section of Río Elba street to meet the parking requirements; by preserving and moving the pre-existing house to the corner of the plot, the project has retained this historical reference to the grand, early-twentieth-century mansions of the Porfirio Díaz era; it is also innovative for its structure and architectural forms. Benjamín Romano, a talented architect and expert in structures and construction processes, displayed his vast knowledge and boundless passion for architecture and the city with this emblematic project. This building, in common with some of his other works, places emphasis on the idea of the triangle as the compositional axis and physical principle of balance, using it in the building's overall floorplan, to articulate corners, as well as in the porous lobby and transparent entrance. The triangle, elevated to a multifaceted volume, creates an auditorium half-way up the building and opens up vistas onto an urban panorama in which Chapultepec Park takes center stage. Romano's structural and compositional control over this geometric form is not gratuitous: he was an outstanding student and follower of Heberto Castillo, the talented and creative engineer who developed the "Tridilosa" construction system based on the use of pyramid-shaped steel structures, considerably decreasing the weight of floor slabs and allowing larger, column-free spaces. I can affirm that every state-of-the-art technology was used for the construction of

Torre Reforma. This factor, combined with its elegance and excellent urban location, is one of its most visible achievements.

Above I referred to Mario Pani's project for the intersection of Reforma and Insurgentes in which the architect envisaged a new city center, a new place where people could gather, away from the Zócalo and the Alameda Central. This was a vision of what would later become a polycentric city. Today, we can confidently state that the result of the "Corredor Turístico Cultural Paseo de la Reforma" masterplan, drawn up and implemented from 2000 to 2004, has succeeded in recovering and renovating this important artery. Thanks to felicitous additions, towers have risen at the junctions between thoroughfares. The Torre Reforma is not an isolated occurrence, but related to a synergy of actions and decisions to occupy a space and exploit its potential in a dignified manner. This tower's neighbors, conceived at a similar time and under comparable circumstances, are the Torre BBVA Bancomer, Torre Chapultepec Uno and the pre-existing Torre Mayor. This set of skyscrapers have made a new mark on the city, turning this area into a flourishing center for offices and services, and use of public spaces.

When we observe the current activities along Paseo de la Reforma, its sidewalks, reservations, walkways and green spaces, whether during weekdays or at weekends, we can exclaim, as appropriate upon the completion of a task or at the end of a battle: Mission accomplished! This urban intervention has successfully and respectfully met the international standard for urban initiatives to create best practice, an area in which our city had previously been found wanting. This pioneering move, designed to inject new life into these urban surroundings, has brought this agenda up to date and made the Mexican capital one of a group of cities that is seeking to become more livable, compact, vertical; with more shared space and better transport and mobility systems. But above all, Mexico City is working to create better public spaces and top-quality architecture.

REGULATIONS

L. BENJAMÍN ROMANO

Applying local building regulations to every project may seem tedious, but we should approach them from a different angle. I see these regulations as a compendium of experiences and knowledge accumulated over time; they allow buildings to function and be on friendly terms with society. Most building codes take their cues from the world's largest cities, with adjustments made to reflect local needs or customs, whether these are the result of environmental factors or other site-specific conditions.

I once visited the Lofoten Islands, located between latitudes 67° and 68° within the Arctic Circle in northern Norway. I was struck by the lack of constructions high up on the hillsides, considering the splendid views on offer from such a vantage point. However, when I mentioned this to a local resident, he explained to me that building was prohibited in that area. I surmised that it must have been an ecological reserve, but the man set me straight: the winds could be so strong, he said, that they would put in danger the lives of anyone living in a building on that higher ground. In this case, regulations exist for safety.

I once had the experience of building in Commerce, California, and I decided to hire the services of a local architect to help me navigate the local building codes. To my surprise, I found that almost all applicable regulations were identical to those in Mexico City, except for some fire-safety regulations as well as disabled-access requirements. And in Israel, for example, specific norms exist for the construction of air-raid shelters, obviously reflecting the conflict in that country.

Ignoring or attempting to circumvent regulations is clearly not only ethically wrong but it also undermines a project's financial viability. In Mexico City, agreements have been detected due to construction companies' building code violations or omissions; after the departure of the corrupt authorities, the incoming administrations have had to close down these projects. For example, the Lomas Plaza Shopping Mall, on Mexico City's *periférico* or beltway known as Boulevard Manuel Ávila Camacho, was built in around 1980 and obviously violated car parking regulations; the problem was not resolved until 2008, when this real-estate investment could finally bear fruit. The financial losses caused by this delay of almost 30 years are incalculable.

Respecting legal regulations works in both directions; citizens not only have obligations but also rights. In 1987, when we were applying for the building permit for Torre Chapultepec, and after receiving the land-use certificate, I received by post a document that revoked it on the express orders of the city's mayor at the time, Ramón Aguirre Velázquez, who, for political motives and under pressure from the chairwoman of the neighborhood committee of Polanco, Dr. Silvia Ortiz de Freyre, decided to issue this revocation of the permit without any legal basis. This forced us to file an *amparo* injunction to defend our constitutional rights as citizens. In the event, Torre Chapultepec was built in accordance with the land-use certificate which we had legally obtained after winning the case. Something similar happened with Gabriela Cuevas, the head of the local district of Miguel Hidalgo, when she refused to grant us the new Construction Certificate (*Manifestación de Construcción*) for Torre Tres Picos. On that occasion, due to the authority's misguided decision, we were forced to visit the local district's offices accompanied by a notary public, who could attest to the arbitrary action by the government, since the authorities are constitutionally required to issue this Certificate when the obligee has fully complied with the relevant legal provisions. Of course, the district authorities eventually provided us the necessary documentation and we began construction.

Torre Reforma was no exception in terms of interpreting the regulation. The first item on our agenda was the listing of the early-20th-century mansion by the National Institute of Fine Arts (INBA) and the Ministry of Urban Development and Housing (SEDUVI). It was obviously never the developers' intention to demolish this grand house, yet even so it proved very difficult to convince the authorities of our noble intentions. While Félix tried to secure the corresponding permits, internally we continued working on a plan about how to move the structure. When we explained the process to the relevant government authorities—our delegation consisted of Roberto Meli, Rodolfo Valles, Enrique Santoyo, Félix and myself—they quickly changed their negative attitude upon seeing the endorsement of the respected professionals working on the project. From that point on, the authorities no longer doubted us and granted the necessary permits. Along with assistance of Jaime Bolaños, we began our analysis of regulatory issues relating to the property, and we were pleasantly surprised when we realized the enormous urban potential in our hands. The specific combination of two building regulations (*Normas de Ordenación*), in addition to the mansion's listed status, determined the project's final design:

> Height = 2 × (separation between opposite alignments + setback + 1.50 m)
>
> All buildings over 6 stories tall must observe a minimum restriction on their rear adjacency of 15 % of their height and a minimum separation of 4 meters.

Since corner plots lack a rear adjacency, the separation requirement was not applicable to our project. The building's urban potential grew considerably when we combined this regulation with the height given to us by the width of Paseo de Reforma.

Furthermore, the preservation of the house enabled us to use that construction's area as unoccupied space, resulting in a building permit that could be classified as a house extension.

Based on our understanding of the regulations, we defined the architectural parti and paid a visit to Arturo Aispuro, Minister of Urban Development, who immediately objected to our interpretation of the regulation, arguing that the permitted height should be calculated only up to a maximum of twice the width of Río Elba street, in other words 40 meters less than Paseo de la Reforma, which clearly ruled out our submitted draft project. Félix, Jaime Bolaños and I were present at the meeting with Arturo. While Jaime and Arturo were arguing their points, I reflected on the suggestive coincidence of a 40-meter frontage with the 40 meters proposed by Arturo, which would form a perfect isosceles triangle. I've always been fascinated by mathematics and even more so by coincidences. The same equation also created a proportion of 6 to 1 for the tower's vertical volume. Without skipping a beat, I replied to Arturo that, although his was a personal interpretation of the regulation, we could adapt to it; however, in return I asked his assurance that there would be no more such personal interpretations. Arturo gave his word and Jaime immediately questioned what I had said, believing that I had misunderstood the seriousness of the difference in the interpretation. Of course I had understood it well, but what Jaime had failed to realize is that Arturo was creating for us a perfect triangular prism, which we would simply have to adapt.

Essentially, the solution for the proposed geometry was to separate the volume of the express elevators. We quickly returned to submit the draft project and it was authorized; Arturo kept his word and did not make any further objections.

I have often been asked where I found the inspiration for the form and volumes of the project, to which I simply reply that I adapted it to the context, the program, the flows, and the regulations.

The interpretation of the building's regulations were as follows:

Location	Reforma No. 483, Colonia Cuauhtémoc, Delegación Cuauhtémoc, Mexico City.
Building type	Extension
Land use	Two zones apply: Multifamily Residence and/or Offices and/or Tourism Services with Ground-Floor Retail Units and "C-type" Residence
Property area	
Merged*:	2,788.21 m²* Reforma No. 483, Colonia Cuauhtémoc, Delegación Cuauhtémoc, Mexico City.

* 5 properties were merged in total.

1. ANALYSIS OF EXISTING REGULATIONS

According to the Certificate of Land-Use Zoning for the property in question, the project includes the following zones: Multifamily Residence and/or Offices and/or Tourism Services with Ground-Floor Retail Units and "C-type" Residence, with a height of up to 6 stories or 18 meters.

After a "Polígono de Actuación"[1] was created through the "Sistema de Actuación Privado,"[2] corresponding to the properties at Paseo de la Reforma 483, and 481, on Río Elba 56 and on Río Atoyac 72 and 68, in the Cuauhtémoc neighborhood of the Cuauhtémoc borough, a single merged property was formed at Paseo de la Reforma 483, categorized under the urban development plans and programs:

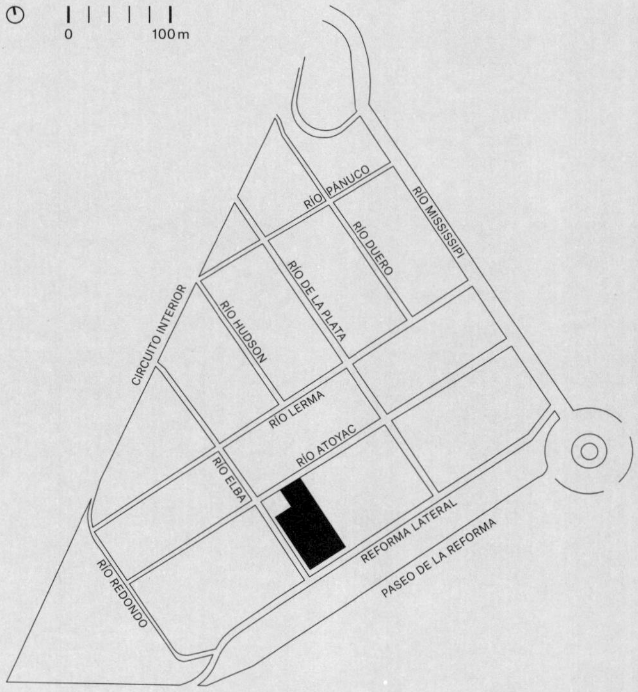

Location of properties
Av. Paseo de la Reforma 483,
Río Elba 56,
Río Atoyac 72 and 68

Total area
2,788.21 m²

Unused area
1,040.08 m², 37.3%

Footprint
1,748.13 m², 62.7%

Maximum built area requested
54,123.99 m²

Plot ratio
19

Levels
8, 10, 13, 32 and 57

No. of residences

2. PROPOSAL OF RELOCATION OF USES AND INTENSITIES

Location of properties
Av. Paseo de la Reforma 483

Total area
2,788.21 m²

Unused area
1,040.08 m², 37.3%

Footprint
1,748.13 m², 62.7%

Maximum built area requested
55,094.30 m²

Plot ratio
19

Levels
13, 13, 32 and 57

No. of residences

1.
A *Polígono de Actuación* is an administrative process for specific projects which involve a reparceling and/or relocation of land usages, on one or more plots, in accordance with the provisions of the Urban Development Programs, the Federal District's Urban Development Law and its applicable regulations, without this altering the regulations on building intensity (m²) and density (number of homes).

2.
A government initiative to join up the work of private sector urban constructions and developments.

3. HEIGHT ANALYSIS

The construction is divided into:

The pre-existing house
The main tower
The express elevator body
The robotic parking facility on Río Elba
The robotic parking facility on Río Atoyac

The mezzanine heights vary in the five bodies, both in regard to one another and internally. Therefore, the following details are provided for each body:

Our project could reach its height since it is formed by a *Polígono de Actuación*, making it possible to achieve the best height as long as it created a larger area of unused space, with an actual footprint of 59.75 % compared to the 76.37% of permitted occupancy according to Colonia Cuauhtémoc's urban development program for the group of properties.

The presence of the pre-existing house allowed us to give 25% of the unused area precisely in the area of the historical building's footprint.

Pre-existing house

LEVELS		
1	Ground floor	5.12 m
1	Top floor	4.61 m
	Maximum height	**9.73 m**

Main tower

LEVELS			
3	Ground-floor lobby	16.80 m	(Triple-height)
6	Gymnasium	25.20 m	(Includes swimming pool)
12	Offices	50.40 m	(Low-rise)
3	Sky Lobby	16.80 m	(Triple-height)
12	Offices	52.40 m	(Mid-rise)
18	Offices	71.40 m	(High-rise)
2	Mechanical rooms	13.00 m	
	Maximum height	**246.00 m**	

Express elevator tower

LEVELS		
1	Ground-floor lobby (double-height)	8.40 m
7	Mechanical rooms	29.75 m
14	Shaft floors	54.25 m
1	Mechanical rooms	7.00 m
1	Sky Lobby	5.60 m
1	Mechanical rooms	4.20 m
6	Mechanical rooms	29.40 m
	Maximum height	**138.60 m**

Robotic parking facility on Río Elba

LEVELS		
1	Ground-floor lobby	8.40 m
1	Mezzanine-Lobby	4.20 m
1	Transfer	2.80 m
1	Transfer	2.80 m
1	Transfer	4.20 m
10	Transfer	2.80 m
	Maximum height	**42.00 m**

Robotic parking facility on Río Atoyac

LEVELS		
1	Mezzanine-Lobby (Half a level above sidewalk)	4.20 m
7	Parking	20.82 m (Lower floors)
2	Parking	5.95 m (Lower floors)
	Maximum height	**30.97 m**

The proposed project uses only 58.34% of the permitted zoning (including all the lots together), therefore the ratio changed from 32.21 (v.a.t.)[3] to 18.79 (v.a.t.) times the lot size. In accordance with the applicable regulations: Colonia Cuauhtémoc's urban development program and its applicable regulations: Federal District Building Code, August 2, 1993.

3.
v.a.t.: Is a ratio between the construction and the lot area

Drawing: Application of the criteria of articles 74 and 75 of the Federal District Building Code of August 2, 1993.

Point A	Height	**Point E**	Height
2×102.00	204.00 m	2×20.00	40.00 m
Point B	Height	**Point F**	Height
2×122.00	246.00 m	2×45.70	91.40 m
Point C	up to setback	**Point G**	Height
2×20.00	40.00 m	2×12.00	24.00 m
Point D	Height	**Point H**	Height
2×142.00	284.00 m	2×15.60	31.20 m

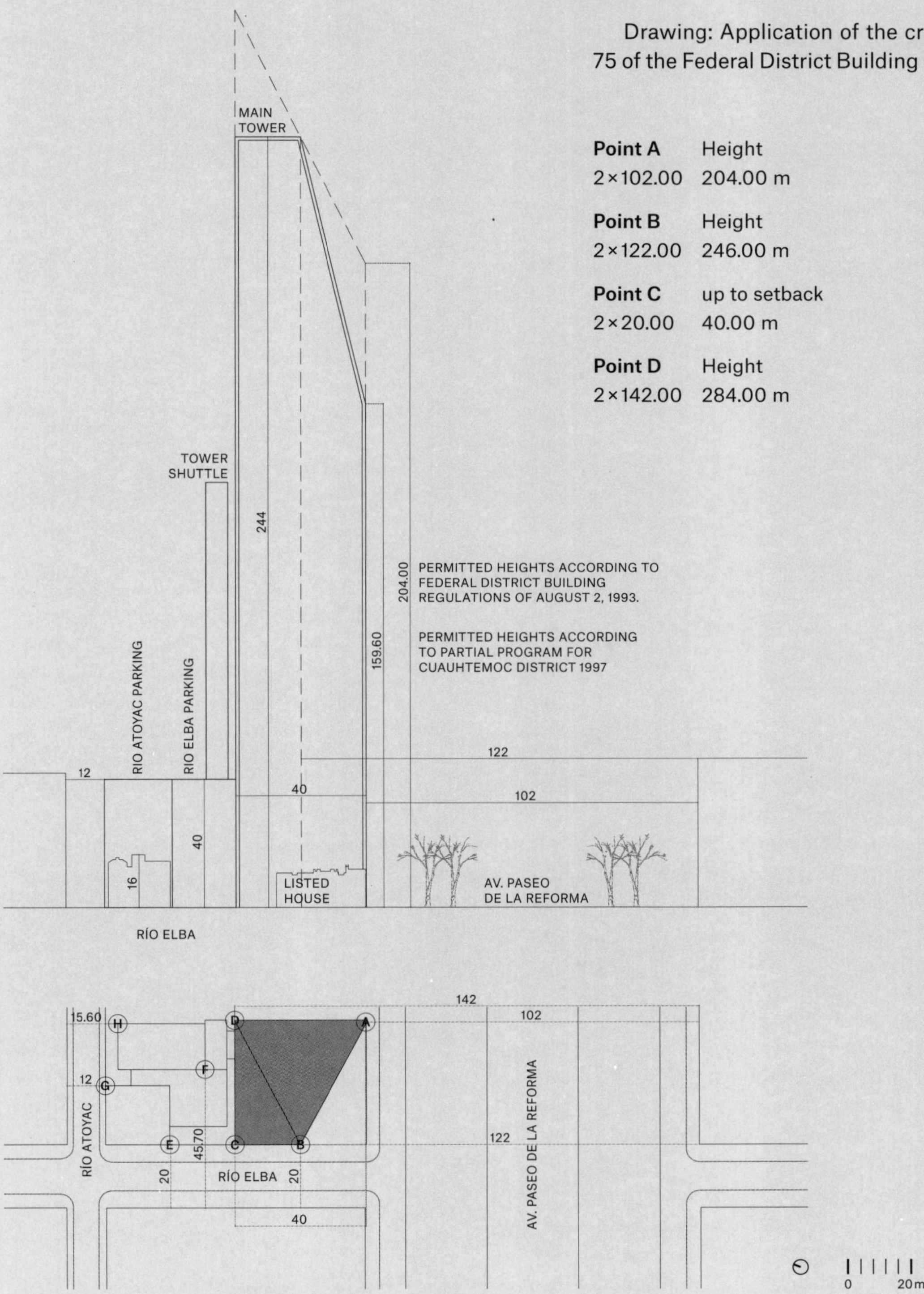

4. PARKING FACILITIES ANALYSIS

ANNEX 1 shows the project's different areas by use, and ANNEX 2 analyzes the quantification of the need in accordance with the Federal District Building Code of August 2, 1993, and the Colonia Cuauhtémoc's urban development program of 1997.

Distribution of car parking spaces in the building

LEVEL	LARGE SPACE	SMALL SPACE	DISABLED SPACES	TOTAL
Basement 1	0	0	-	0
Basement 2	11	30	-	41
Basement 3	19	45	-	64
Basement 4	27	53	-	80
Basement 5	28	53	-	81
Basement 6	28	53	-	81
Basement 7	28	53	-	81
Basement 8	28	53	-	81
Basement 9	29	50	-	79
Raised parking area 1–26	424	0	424*	424
Total	**622**	**390**		**1,012**
Porcentaje	62%	38%		100%

* Disabled people can use all spaces on the upper levels of the parking facilities.

The total demand offers 1,012 spaces for 973 users.

List of administrative documents and permits obtained for the development of the project:

Street alignment and official number (*Alineamiento y Número Oficial*), Certificate of land-use zoning (*Certificado único de Zonificación de Uso del Suelo*), Proof of no outstanding water / housing tax bills (*Constancia de No Adeudo Agua/Predial*), Special demolition permit (*Licencia de Construcción Especial para Demolición*), Special construction permit for protective barriers (*Licencia de Construcción Especial para Tapiales*), Special excavation permit (*Licencia de Construcción Especial para Excavación*), Tree felling and/or pruning permit / Urban Services Department of Cuauhtémoc Borough (*Tala y/o Derribo de Árboles / Dirección General de Servicios Urbanos Cuauhtémoc*), Installation of Ecological Nursery 2009–2011 / Urban Services Department of Cuauhtémoc Borough (*Instalación de Vivero Ecológico 2009–2011 / Dirección General de Servicios Urbanos Cuauhtémoc*), Property merging (*Fusión de Predios*), Cultural heritage approval for demolition (*Visto Bueno de Patrimonio Cultural para la Demolición*), Cultural heritage approval for moving listed building (*Visto Bueno de Patrimonio Cultural para el Movimiento de Casona*), Cultural heritage approval for excavation (*Visto Bueno de Patrimonio Cultural para la Excavación*), Cultural heritage approval for new construction (*Visto Bueno de Patrimonio Cultural para Obra Nueva*), INBA approval for demolition (*Visto Bueno de INBA para la Demolición*), INBA approval for excavation (*Visto Bueno de INBA para la Excavación*), INBA approval for new construction (*Visto Bueno de INBA para Obra Nueva*), SEDUVI environment impact analysis (*Impacto Ambiental SEDUVI*), SEDUVI urban impact analysis (*Impacto Urbano SEDUVI*), SEDUVI'S "Polígono de Actuación" (*Polígono de Actuación SEDUVI*), Revocable Temporary Permit (PATR) for temporary use of Río Elba (*Permiso Administrativo Temporal Revocable para el uso temporal de Río Elba*), Feasibility of water supply from Mexico City's water authority (*Factibilidad de Servicios por parte del Sistema de Aguas de la Ciudad de México*), Zero-discharge certificate from Mexico City's water authority (*Descarga Cero por parte del Sistema de Aguas de la Ciudad de México*), Alternative rainwater harvesting system (*Sistema Alternativo de Aprovechamiento de Agua Pluvial*), Technical parking facility design, Secretary of Mobility (*Proyecto Ejecutivo del Estacionamiento Secretaría de Movilidad*), Work completion notification (*Aviso de Terminación de Obra*), Authorization of use (*Autorización de Uso y Ocupación*), Structural safety certificate (*Aviso de Constancia de Seguridad Estructural*), Operational and safety certificate (*Aviso de Visto Bueno de Seguridad y Operación*), Sole environmental licence (*Licencia Ambiental Única*) and Approval of the internal civil protection plan (*Aprobación del Programa Interno de Protección Civil*).

STRUCTURE

L. BENJAMÍN ROMANO

When my friends question me about the decision to hire ARUP, I respond with a comment I made to the investors: "If they can save me a kilo for each square meter of construction, then I'm sure their fee—whatever it may be—would be a gift."

Of course, I understand that my response should have been far more analytical, since I am sure that Arup's experience goes far beyond a simple fee or a possible saving in tons of steel.

In short, with the exception of one unfortunate event, our working relationship was outstanding and to the highest standard of professionalism.

I asked to work with the engineer Cecil Balmond on the concept design, and so Walter and I met several times in Mexico City and at the Advanced Geometry Unit (AGU) in London. Soon after presenting the parti, Cecil came to Mexico with a supposed engineering model but surprised us with a completely different architectural proposal.

His brazen idea of becoming Torre Reforma's architect failed; we dismissed him immediately from the meeting and presented a formal complaint to Arup's Head Office in the United States, and they took the matter very seriously. I am unaware why Cecil Balmond left ARUP, but since then he has no longer worked for the company.

IN THIS WORLD OF SKYSCRAPERS, BEWARE OF THE SHARKS...

Our work with ARUP left us with significant experiences in every area, although it is worth mentioning a number of solutions that were achieved in a Mexican style, in a simple and different sense.

When we received the first version of the structural concept, the engineer in charge decided to alter our structural parti and swapped the concrete walls for columns and metal diagonals clad in prefabricated elements that would resemble the building's tectonics.

At the end of the presentation I angrily told this engineer that I would certainly have failed him if he had been my student, if only for making my structure work with the heavy and sterile load of prefabricated elements.

Heberto Castillo taught me to "eliminate all heavy elements from structures that do not contribute to the structural performance," and also told me "if a non-structural element was needed," then it needed to be "as slender and light as possible," or put to work "so it's not just there being lazy."

Removing the concrete walls would require the metal structures to bear the extra horizontal loads and the use of seismic dampers.

Mexico City has suffered badly from earthquakes and we have seen how structures have proved more resilient.

Unlike traditional skyscrapers in other parts of the world, Torre Reforma is adapted to the Valley of Mexico's particular geology, featuring a typology entirely suited to the local context.

While the idea of using concrete walls was being studied, Walter and I spent our days begging engineering firms in New York for a positive opinion, and I have to confess that none would open their doors to us.

I remember that after the building was completed, an engineering firm came to visit it and questioned why it had not been asked to participate. I confirmed that we had in fact paid them a visit but they were one of the firms that had declined to receive us.

When Moisés and I met with ARUP's regional director, David Scott, he enthusiastically approved of how the strange structural-architectural design had eliminated the need for seismic dampers while also considerably reducing the amount of structural steel used in the building.

The parti generated highly valuable information for ARUP, for the company managing the project, and for us, because using concrete walls substantially reduced the construction expenses in several areas, including the cost of foundations and façades.

Thanks to its design, Torre Reforma required only 76 kilograms of structural steel per square meter, whereas the average amount needed for similar buildings also designed by ARUP for Mexico City is around 130 kilograms.

In March 2016, the American Council of Engineering Companies of New York (ACEC) awarded Torre Reforma the distinction as the best structure designed in that period, thanks to its impressive structural efficiency.

Ricardo Pittella and Tabitha Tavolaro were responsible for the project's overall development, with the support of Rodolfo Valles and Ismael Vásquez in Mexico.

Our experience with Tabitha was very interesting thanks

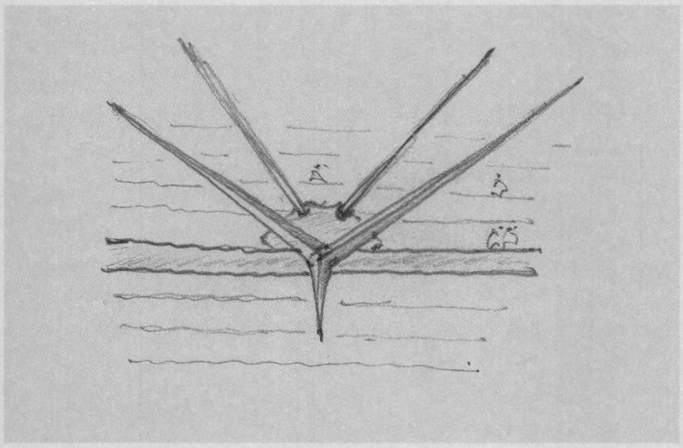

Sketch of structure

to her professionalism and readiness to understand our design, our interests, and above all our way of working in Mexico.

Tabitha and Julieta set about transforming the architectural draft project into an executive project, a process that lasted until the construction documents were complete, a period during which we learned much from the construction logic of ARUP, Mexico, Tabitha, and from construction processes.

A prime example was the constructors' understanding of the kinking of the diagonals in the structure: incredible as it may seem, the structure's twist demands an imperceptible kinking in the line of the diagonal elements, and this had to be taken into account in COREY's preparation of its plans.

Another Mexican contribution to the project occurred when Tabitha presented us with her first proposal for the foundations. I noticed that it included 196 piles, connected with a system of foundation walls and a baseplate, connected to the diaphragm walls that we needed to use for excavating the nine basement levels.

When I received the proposal, I spoke to Rodolfo Valles to share my ideas on my experience with the Torre Chapultepec. Heberto had created the foundations by using a substitution method, without using any piles.

In a simple mathematical operation—dividing the cubic meters of soil extracted by the tower's total weight—Rodolfo eliminated, in theory, all of the proposed piles and foundation walls.

Of course, we discussed the issue with Tabitha and they asked us to validate our idea with an on-site analysis of soil mechanics using a "sonda suspendida."

Time was of the essence because CIMESA needed to start manufacturing the piles, and the "sonda suspendida" available in Mexico was out of order. Félix went into action and managed to bring the equipment down from Texas to speed up the analysis. In the end, all the piles could be eliminated from the project, shaving off more than 7% from the project's total budget.

Another Mexican idea that helped with the project was the use of Heberto Castillo's *tridilosa* pyramid-slab concept for the building slabs. When I proposed this system, given the lack of texts in English to back it up, I invited the engineer Federico Alcaraz Lozano to New York to explain the design theory and method. At the meeting, David Scott asked for more bibliographical references, but Federico responded politely that, apart from the version in Spanish, he was the only existing resource available to them.

At our following meeting, Tabitha confirmed to us that she was astonished at the economy and efficiency of the *tridilosa* system, and that they had decided to employ pyramid beams for Torre Reforma.

A curious anecdote is how the company responsible for producing the metal structure complained during the construction process about the low quote they had given. They had imagined that the company managing the project had calculated the volumes incorrectly, and were sure that we would end up ordering the amount of steel normally required. In their opinion, they sold us and transported "air," which is precisely the structural advantage of pyramid beams (*tridilosa*).

As with every project, the iterations with the engineers are an obligatory part of the process. In our original proposal, we assumed that the ground-floor walls could bear the weight of the building's horizontal loads and we never thought of lowering the façade's diagrid to the ground floor.

Tabitha suggested that the diagrid reach to the bottom of the walls, in order to control the forces, but her idea would block the access to plaza entrance. Walter, Rodolfo and I submitted many proposals, including a good idea to widen the base of the walls on the lower floors, taking advantage of the separation from the adjacency—one meter at ground-floor level—but it was not accepted due to the resulting excess of horizontal forces.

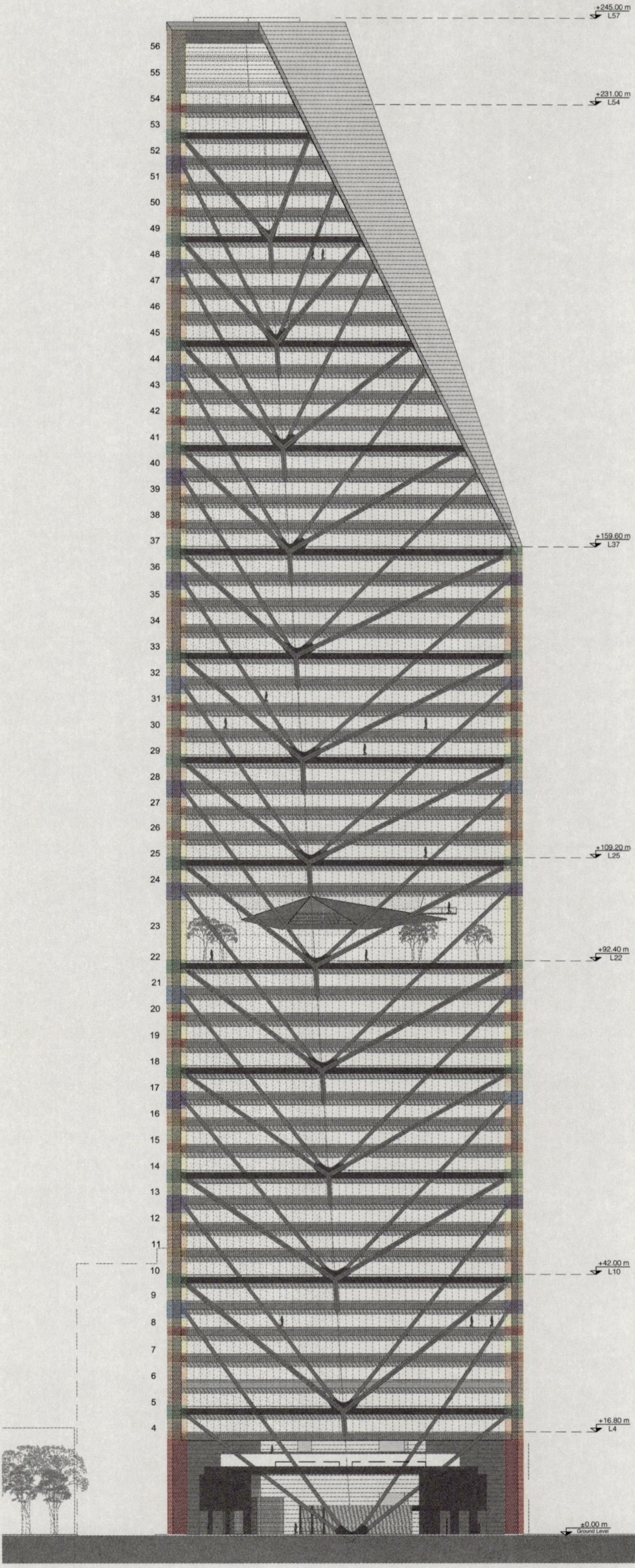

Connector diagrams

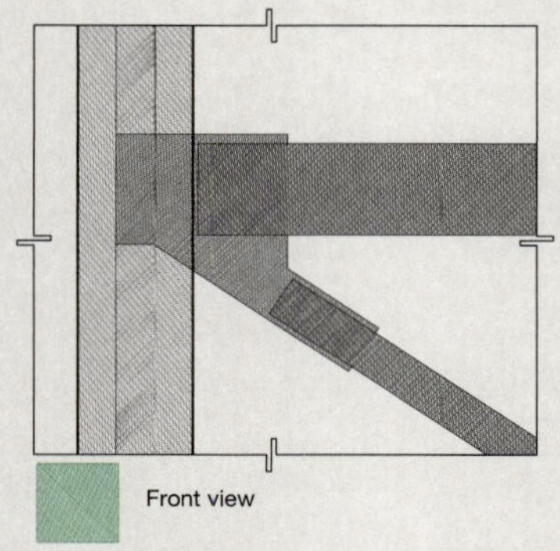

Front view

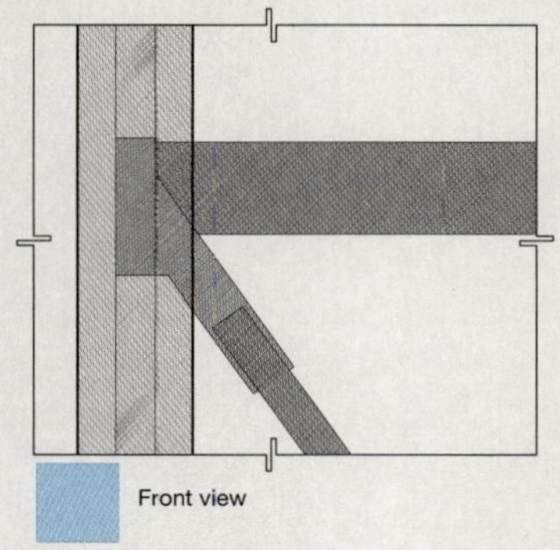

Front view

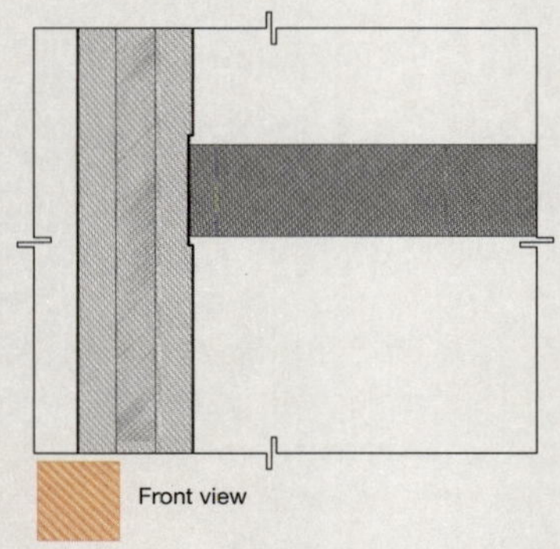

Front view

Rotation in border beam in the glass façade

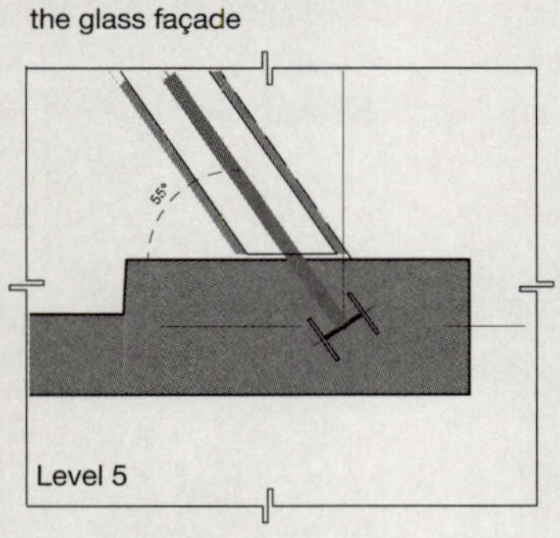

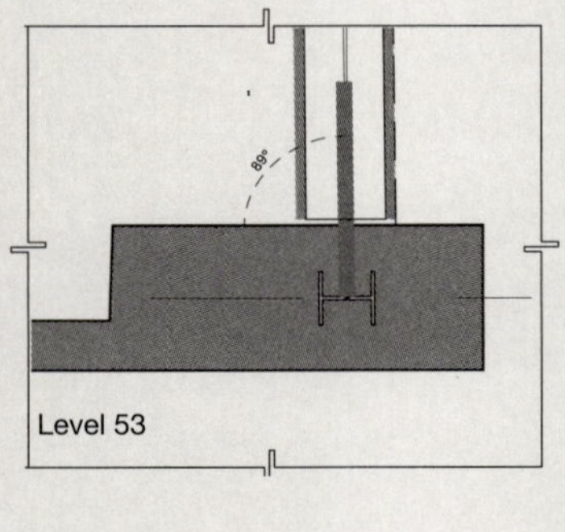

ARUP's rejection led us to analyze the best location to lower the diagrid. We realized that the sloping vertex of the intersection of the south façade coincided perfectly with the intersection between the axis of the hypotenuse and the central axis of the basements. When talking about structures in my classes, I always refer to the importance of seeking to make one axis coincide with another, and another, and so on... and in this case the solution arose by simply making the axes coincide.

The idea delighted Tabitha and she designed a sculptural, structural connection, one I decided to leave exposed. During one of Francisco Serrano and Susana García's many visits to the building, they remarked that this element revealed how the structure was designed.

Another issue that gave rise to many iterations was the design of the gusset plates connecting the diagonals, the concrete walls, and the central nodes of each cluster. In the original proposal, these plates looked like huge oars, and since they affected the proportion of the façade, we once again went through numerous iterations.

Understanding the imaginary yield line was the solution to the architectural design of the gusset plates. With the help of Chucho, Julieta, Rodolfo, Ismael and Tabitha, we could improve the proportions of everything. One curious and innovative element was the use of connecting reinforcements nicknamed *curitas* or "Band-Aids," a solution proposed by Ismael and Rodolfo. These so-called *curitas* are gusset connection plates welded onto the tensioners to meet the additional need for steel.

The proposal for the exposed diagrid on the south façade was the subject of much debate, due to the small eccentricities generated at their connection points. Obviously, the engineers voiced their concern about the increased construction costs; for this reason we requested a financial study before taking any decision.

However, the possibility of creating flexible, divisible office spaces in addition to the extra cost of manufacturing the window frames due to the loss of the repetitive module on the façade, struck me as more important than the extra cost of the relative eccentricity, so I immediately authorized the small increase this made to the budget.

I think it is important to approach the issue of solutions and budgets holistically.

The total cost of the building is important, and not the individual solutions that seem to offer a saving but consequently create extra costs in other areas.

CONCRETE WALL

The understanding of the concrete wall as both façade and structure was a decision that I had to take very seriously, due to its appearance and the complexity of its execution. Within the urban context, its texture and quality had to be excellent, and in terms of its interior, it had to be impeccable. The constructors had difficulty understanding this twofold quality. They repeated their assurance about the quality of its exterior quality, but we were also concerned

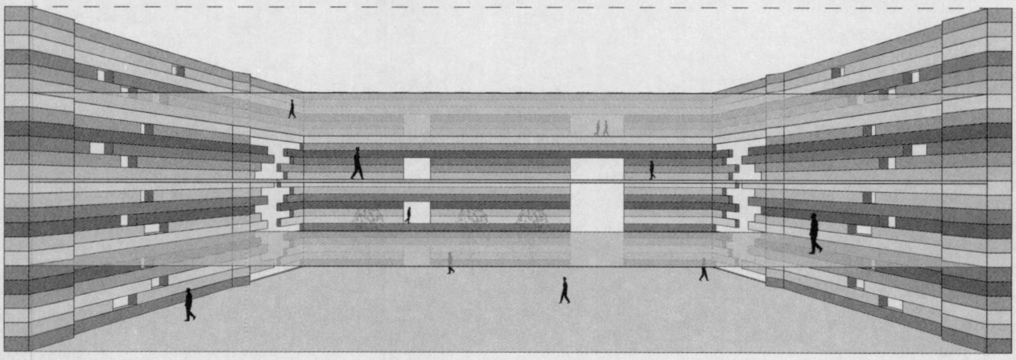

Cluster

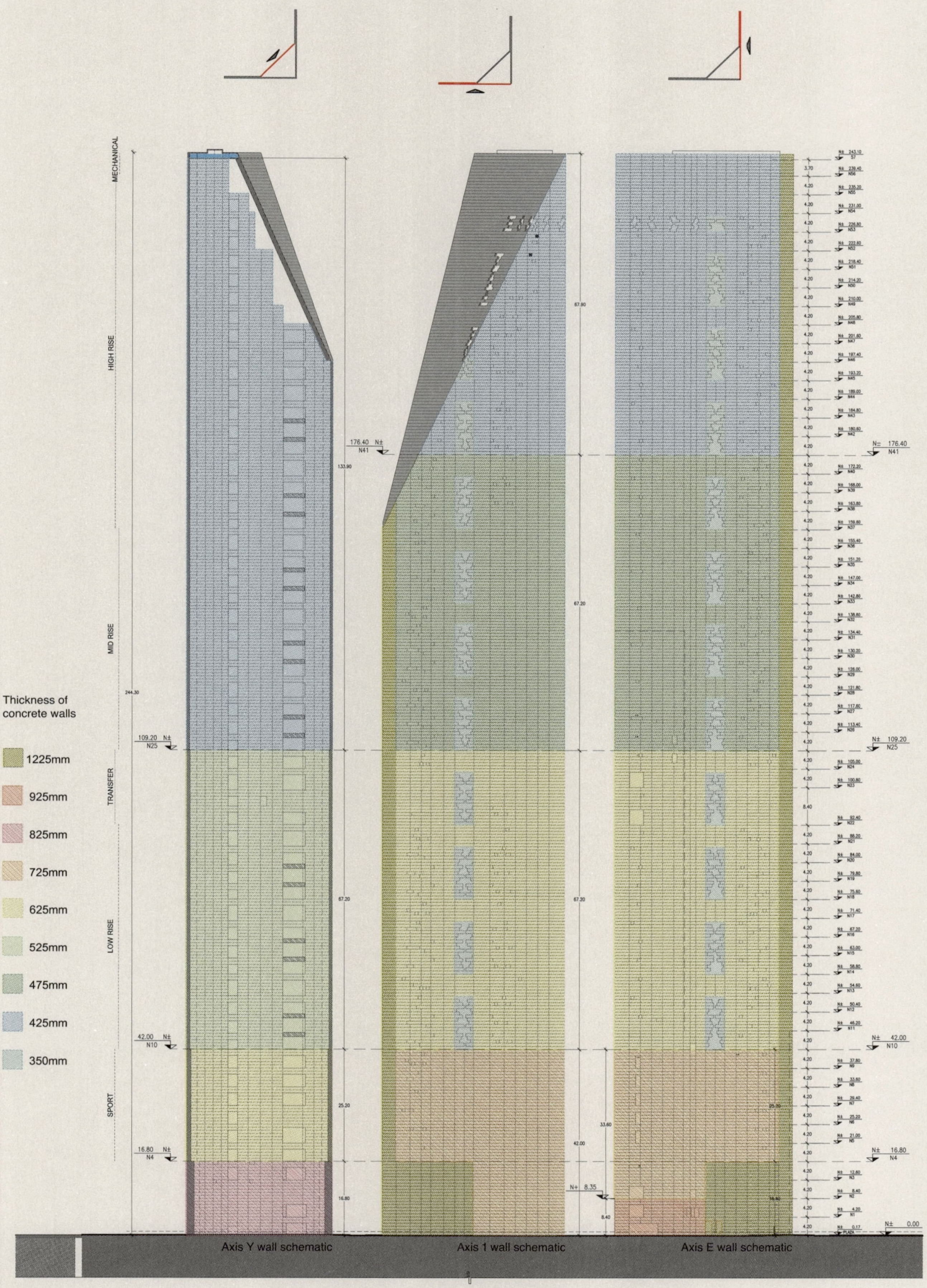

Thickness of the concrete wall

0 15m

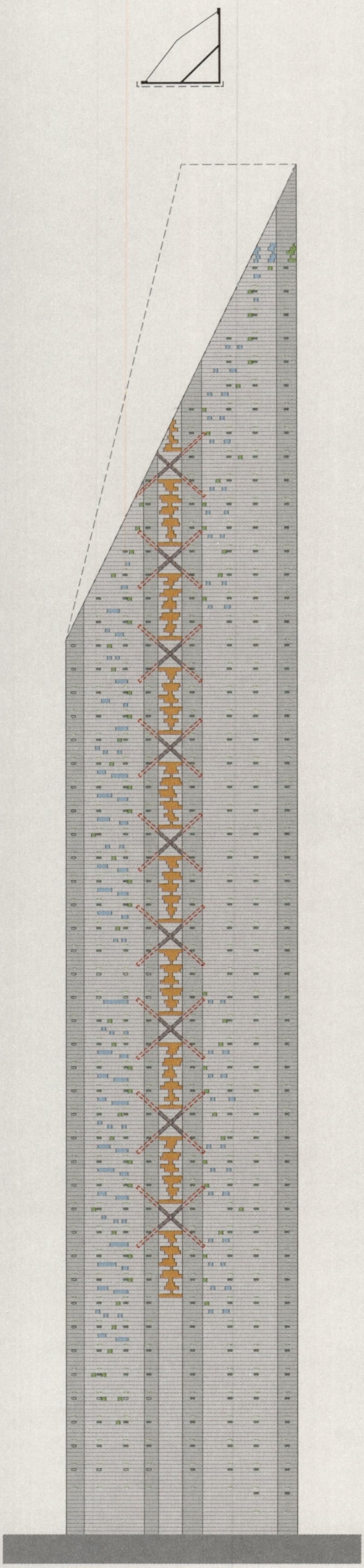

Elevation wall Axis 1

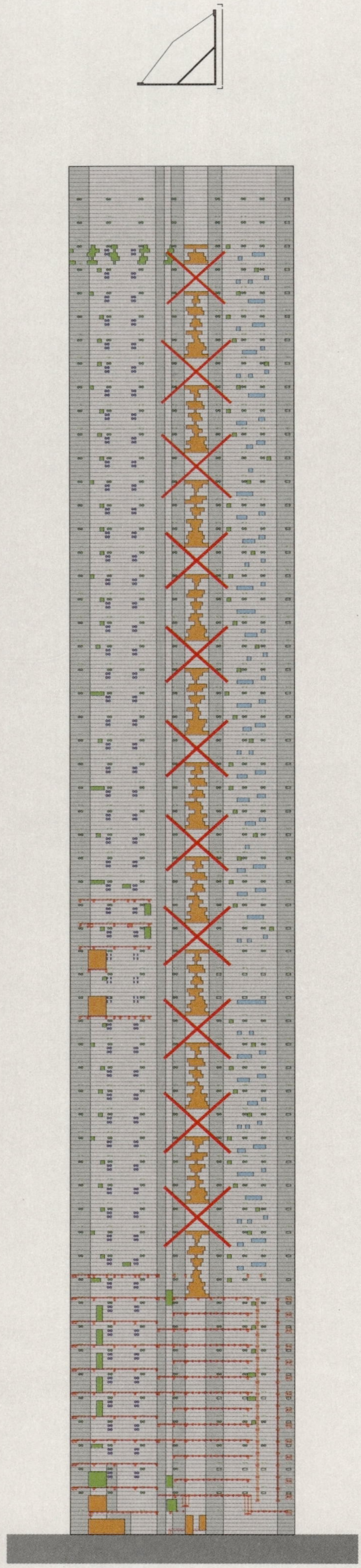

Elevation wall Axis E

KEY

- Opening for passageway or patios
- Window openings
- Openings for services and installations
- indicative — Power Tower EFCO (Coil anchor)
- indicative — Power Tower EFCO (Holemaker)
- Push Beam EFCO
- indicative — Pump Frame EFCO (Nut box)
- indicative — Pump Frame EFCO (Holemaker)
- Structural elements in wall

with the finish of the interior space. Hence Harón and Mario had the job of "ensuring twofold quality." Mario developed the plans for the wall details, recording all the information about the architecture, formwork and connections of each one of the walls.

The density of the steel in the concrete wall also presented major construction challenges, which were largely resolved with the use of extruded connectors or bulbs. However, we had a very interesting situation with the intersection of the X-shaped metal coupling beams. These beams are embedded in the concrete walls, and the original proposal was to receive these forces with the rebar, but not even bulbs were sufficient for the density of steel required. With the assistance of the BIM model, Rodolfo and Ismael suggested an atypical connection, designed with four-inch-thick steel plates with soldered connections.

Given the dimensions of the metalwork—each measuring three levels—the design had to take into account the deformations of its own weight and the possibility of a seismic event while the concrete was being poured; therefore, some temporary columns were embedded into the wall, which alongside the final X-shaped column axis gave temporary stability to the element. The impressive assembly of the metalwork—23 elements in total—always surprised us, due to their ductility and immense size resulting from the manufacture.

The rusticated texture of the wall resulted from something I noticed while walking the streets of Paris with Rosi. On that trip, I noted that the buildings with grooved masonry aged better than buildings that use smooth ashlar, and that the jointing hides and softens the decoloring and staining. Concerned about the appearance of the exposed concrete wall, and aware that pouring errors were inevitable as well as variations in color (due to the varying humidity and mix on each day) I decided to divide the process into monolithic pours, each one 70 centimeter deep, assuming that there would be a "lollipop" effect of the wall's texture, nuanced by the construction process.

As Peter Zumthor said: "the true essence of architecture lies in the act of construction."

Good formwork, correct pouring and vibrating, a proper specification of concrete and use of form release agents, are all well known, but the correct handling of temperature when removing the formwork is something we had

The grooves in the stonework tone down the colors of the stone. Paris, 2010.

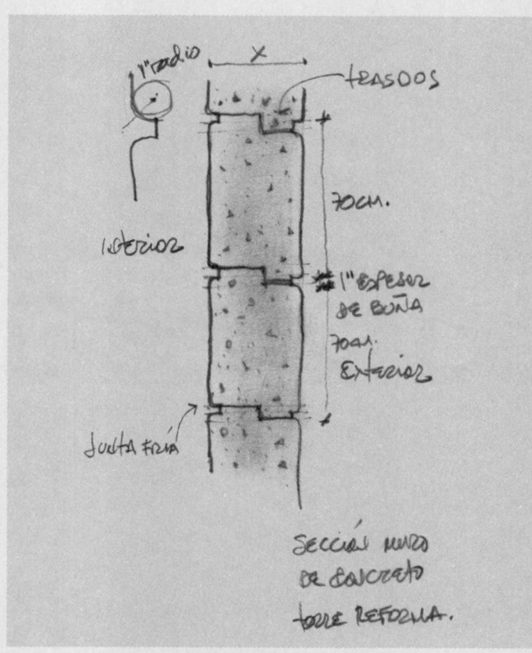

Cross-section of concrete wall

Seismogram

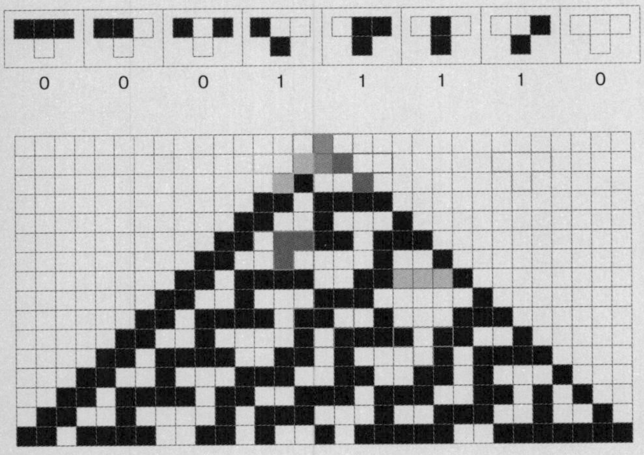

Parameters used in Grasshopper

never heard about. From some Swiss advice obtained by Pablo, we discovered that concrete, when freed from the formwork, receives a thermal shock due to the difference between its own temperature—which is the product of the chemical reaction—and the surrounding atmospheric conditions.

The cold mornings in Mexico City would produce a thermal shock that could lead to cracks on the concrete's surface, and so we were advised to minimize the effect by installing tarpaulin curtains to create a microclimate closer to the interior temperature of the poured concrete.

The design for the concrete wall construction process was the subject of countless meetings with the makers of the formwork, the Swiss advisor, and the Cemex experts. One of the crucial issues was how to induce the cracks in the concrete. Heberto taught me that to channel cracks you needed to avoid areas of concrete larger than 10 square meters. The chosen modulation of 70-centimeter courses, multiplied by six pours totaled 4.2 meters of height for each level, a modulation that in turn represented four stairs of 17.5 centimeters, resulting in a series of slices (or pours) of 70 centimeters in an A-shape (in plan view), with 40-meter sides, which we divided into sections with a maximum area of 10 square meters. Horizontally, the cold pouring joints worked perfectly, and we requested vertical grooves spaced less than the 10 meters apart, as recommended by Heberto. The groove in the formwork was misunderstood by the manufacturers, who proposed a one-inch thickness for the grooves, which spoiled the whole horizontal effect we were looking to create. We realized this during the pouring tests and quickly asked for a change, resulting in an elegant triangular groove narrowing from 3 mm on the outer edge, down to 0 mm at the tip.

We had always intended the concrete to be Oxford gray, but when we carried out pouring tests with the commercial minerals we were surprised to see that the pigment's mineral composition reacted with the centrifugal movement of the vibrator and produced black stains on the contact surface. Our advisors recommended us to omit the vibrating, but ARUP insisted that we should. We decided to prioritize structural security over the visual appearance of the concrete.

Carrying out the final pouring test, we asked to use

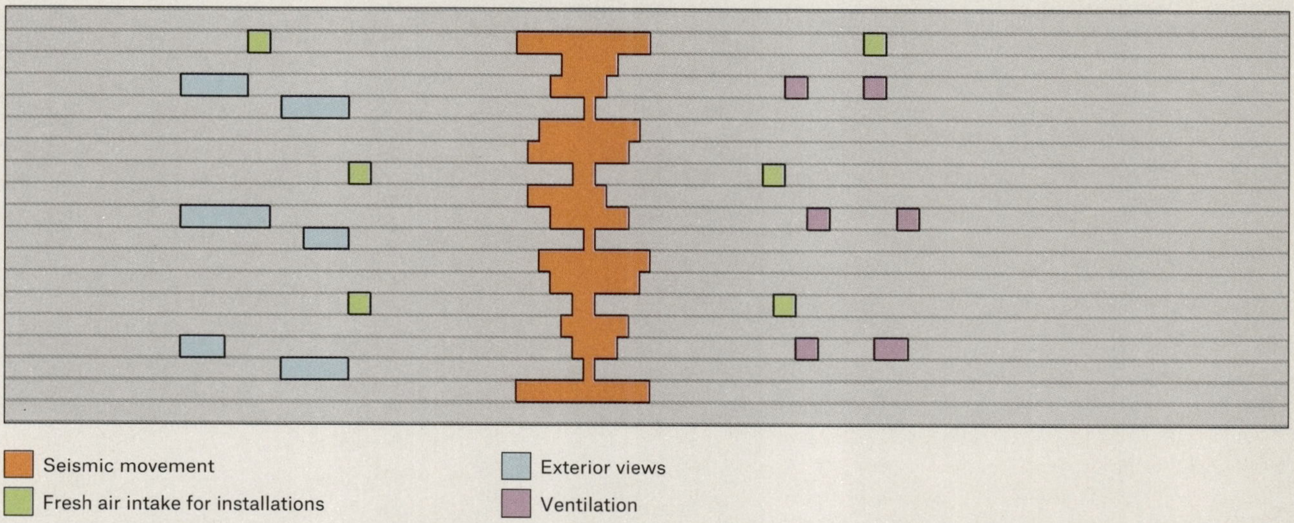

Design parameters for the concrete wall

exactly the same concrete that we had specified—f'c 500—and were surprised to see that the high-resistance concrete produced a much darker tone. We left the test very excited about the result of the expected formwork, color and quality of the pour. I remember that our constant visits to the Cemex plant made the security staff nervous whenever they saw us, as they could not understand why we were turning up so frequently for a single project. Their vigilance increased with each subsequent visit.

The well-chosen formwork design, bracing, guttering and outer facing to prevent water from seeping into the buildings are visible in each section and allow the wall to perform well in case of wind, rain, or earthquakes.

Tabitha defined for us a number of structural design parameters for the wall; together with the openings required for visual purposes, mechanical requirements, habitability and the construction process itself, these create the concrete walls' final appearance.

I have sometimes been asked if the design of the apertures reflects a Maya or Aztec hieroglyph. The fact is that every single opening in the walls exists for a specific reason and is designed parametrically based on the building's 70-cm modulation, reasons of habitability, mechanics, structure and construction processes. This gave rise to a unique, unrepeatable pattern, which has been nicknamed "Tetris" after the computer game. A careful analysis of the building in detail reveals some of the patterns generated by the design. In my view the clearest one may be seen in the "Tetris" on the north façade, where an opening appears in the first four courses, created to provide an entry point for materials during the construction process.

MOVING THE HOUSE

When I was invited to visit the property before buying it, I was asked about my plans for the listed house. Full of excitement, I answered that the new building would be great and that I would decide what to do with the pre-existing house. However, when starting out with the project, we ran into the problem of the excessive number of car parking spaces required by the regulations. Therefore, I took the decision to move the house to create underground parking levels.

The idea was great, we just needed to find a way to do it.

At the time the house was being used as a bar-nightclub and they allowed us to use the premises for our meetings. Roberto Meli, Enrique Santoyo, Rodolfo and I were discussing the problem until I remember one day observing the tray from the night before, stacked with empty bottles and glasses. At that point I realized that a similar type of tray could be used to move the house. Everyone was excited by the idea. We immediately ordered a test cut to be made near the foundations in order to learn how we could manufacture the "tray."

We proposed using a diamond-cutting disc to pass a rebar cage in two directions to encase the house's original foundations in concrete. The perforations in the original foundations were based on the width of the slab's ribbing.

When I told people in the studio about the idea of moving the house, Diego looked online about the process used to move the roof of the stadium in Athens for the Olympics: the stadium's construction was significantly delayed, and given the time pressure they decided to build the roof at the same time as the stadium and then moved it to cover the stadium in time.

We used the same people to move the house as the ones who undertook the maneuver in Athens. The idea turned out to be easier and less expensive than we had thought, although I will never forget the expressions of incredulity of one of the investors when I suggested the idea of temporarily moving the house.

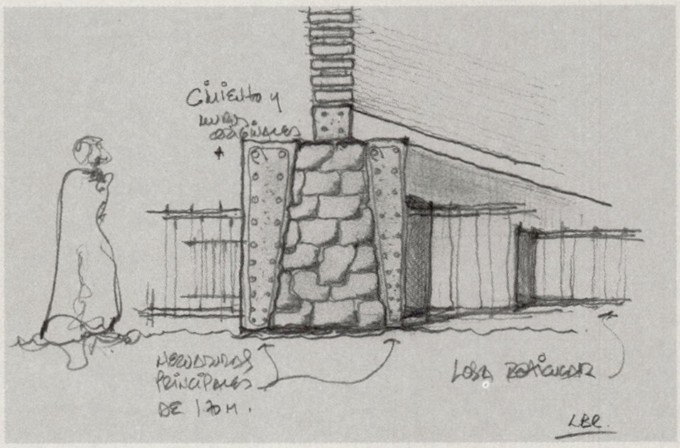

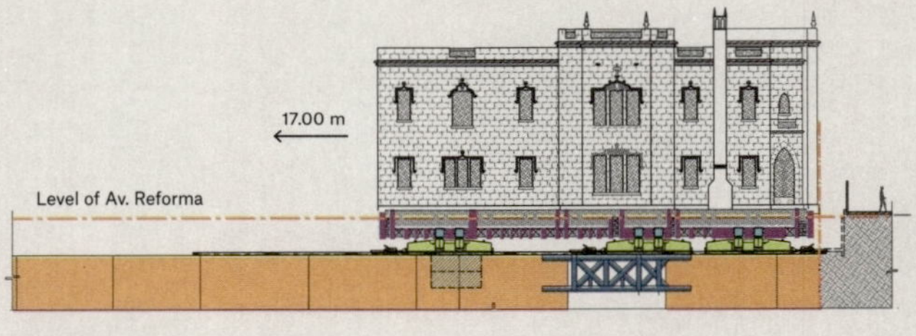

Phase 1

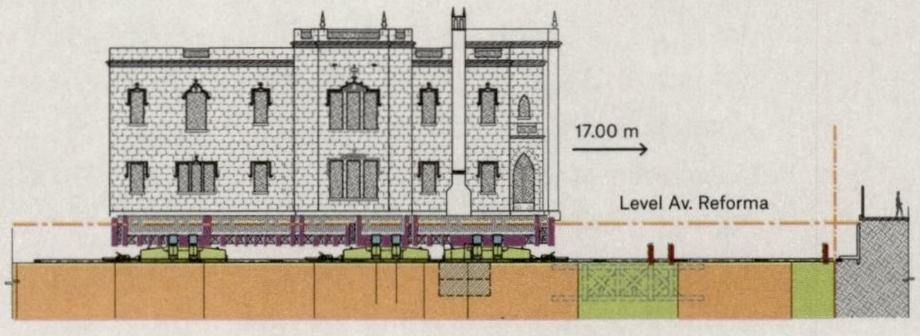

Phase 2

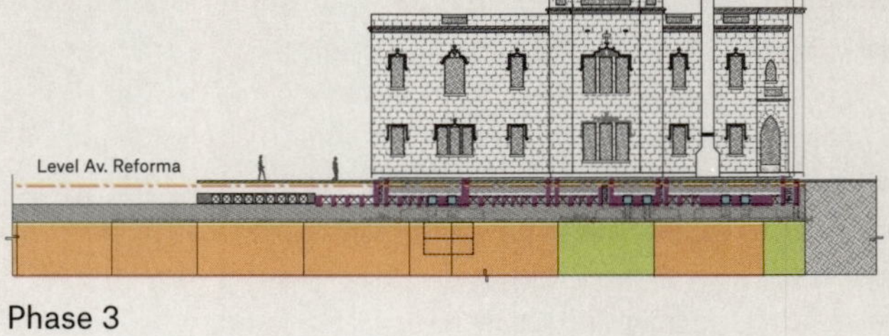

Phase 3

Roberto Meli, Rodolfo Valles, Ismael Vázquez, Julieta Boy, Antonella Morritu, César Balmes, Pablo Duro and L. Benjamín Romano discussing the preparation of the house.

Phase 1

Phase 2

FLOWS

L. BENJAMÍN ROMANO

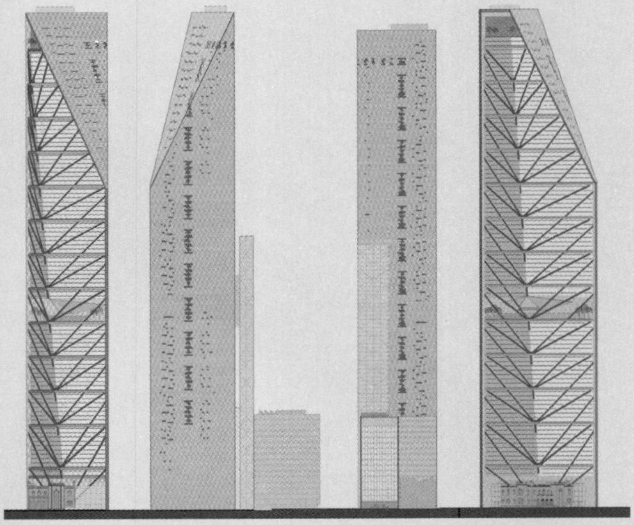

Façades

In defining the architectural parti, different elements must be taken into account: site and program, exposure to wind and sun, light, views both to and from the site, as well as the different flows that will coexist in the building, as all of them influence the parti that determines the project. Architecture critics consider that a good understanding and interpretation of the architectural parti is synonymous with a good living space, a successful integration in the urban context, and favorable and balanced flows.

In this regard, it is important to clarify that in an architectural project there are flows of different kinds: structural ones, which carry the load through the building to the ground; pedestrian or vehicular; power; telecommunications; water, wastewater and drainage; wind and insolation. When the flows combine correctly in the space, the resulting volume acquires a logical and proportional scale, with a unique personality and aesthetic, which some people describe as beautiful and functional.

The importance of an adequate design of the flows of a space can easily be understood if we analyze the flows inside a living being. For example, in the human body, the complexity and individuality of the trajectory of the different flows, produced by the evolution of the species—that is, of the iterations—are comparable to the successful design of flows in buildings. In the human body the flow of the bone structure coexists with the flow of sensations, awareness and communication, which in turn are clearly distinct from the digestive functions—food and waste—and oxygenation and chemical functions. All maintain a marvelous coordination and individuality. When there is a natural or accidental malformation, the bodily function inevitably degrades, giving rise to a poor quality of life and possible deterioration of the physical appearance. In the field of architecture, when the flow of users in the space is incorrect, or when the trajectory of the flows faces operational problems, then we may say the building suffers malformations.

In our constant search to imitate nature and everyday living elements to apply them to architectural solutions, we understand that the architectural parti for Torre Reforma should be defined by three walls of exposed concrete, arranged in the form of an open book, with a spinal canal to the rear designed to accommodate the servant space. This canal allows the building's flows to function in a correct, individual manner, and is clearly distinguished from the served space—habitable space—which is located to the front of the building to take advantage of the dominant views over Chapultepec Park. These walls shape the building, forming and containing the volume, support the weight of the structure, receive much of the seismic forces and transmit the load of the building to the ground, working as frictional foundation elements. The third façade is formed by 14 independent pairs of tensioned steel elements that transfer loads to the loadbearing walls and form the structural diagrid. The system of diagonal tensors is responsible for the horizontal and vertical stresses of the glass façade and forms the same number of clusters, each consisting of four floors. The individuality of the diagonal tensors allows this façade to rotate in search of the best views over the Bosque de Chapultepec, while also increasing the rentable area of the upper floors. This rotation in the façade generates a cantilever of 14 meters over the preserved historical building that is embraced by the entrance lobby. To preserve this mansion, it was necessary to temporarily displace it by a distance of 14 meters, in order to be able to excavate a larger basement, as a way of meeting the disproportionate local requirement for parking spaces.

The clarity and strength of the architectural elements makes it possible for the project to incorporate the building's spatial and functional design in a single concept, defined solely by the three large walls.

The served space of offices and other facilities, with its striking views of the Chapultepec Park, offers a unique spatial character due to the absence of structural columns. The lack of columns allows users to freely adapt their office space and the building's sports and retail spaces. The elimination of columns has been an important goal of LBR&A projects. It has been achieved by understanding façades as construction elements between inside and

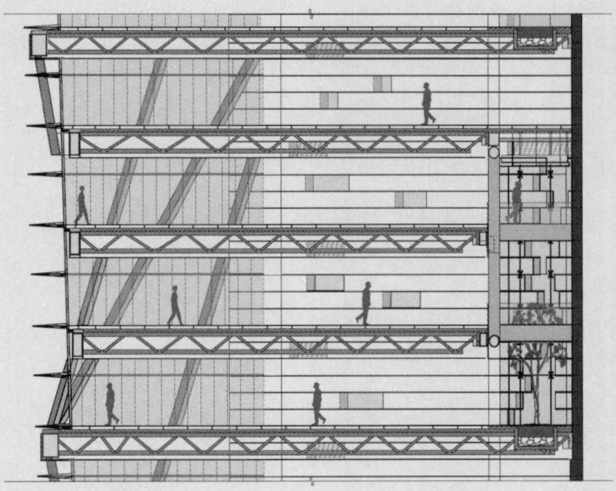

Landscaped patios

outside, rather than as large and sterile loads that demand additional structures which increase the cost of buildings.

Another concept of Mexican origin that was incorporated into the building is the triple-height gardened atria, providing for cross-ventilation. Each cluster of four floors has its own private garden for people to relax in, designed with natural light and ventilation, and which penetrates the space through the openings in the concrete walls. The structure of the walls and the triple-height atria is designed to allow flexing in the concrete walls in the event of a seismic event, which serves to liberate energy. The fourth floor of each cluster acts as a structural belt to integrate the building's served and servant spaces.

The atria are the conduct through which the mechanical extraction equipment evacuates the stale air of the offices during the night, providing further energy efficiency.

To understand the flow of winds around the building, a computational fluid dynamics study was carried out at the University of Pennsylvania, with the following results, as illustrated overleaf.

Each cluster works with its own compartmentalized mechanical, electric and plumbing (MEP) program, which improves efficiency of flows. Six electrical substation transformers were installed in the building to convert 23,000 volts into 480 volts, and 14 smaller transformers were installed in each cluster to convert 480 volts into 220 volts, minimizing the size of the electrical conductor and maximizing the conductor's efficiency by reducing voltage losses. The generators were designed to supply 23,000 volts, which means that the redundant double electrical network can be used when there is a power cut, a common problem in Mexico City.

Voice and data services are transmitted by two independent vertical conduits. One is used for security purposes—aligned with a series of totems—controlling the elevators, fire safety and access; the other conduit handles the building and the digital communications systems of the occupants.

The water tanks are installed in three different locations. This minimizes the use of energy for water pumps and guarantees the demand for gravity-fed drinking water, as well as its availability in event of a fire. A compartmentalized system of water tanks in the lowest basement manages the drinking, raw, rain and recycled water that is pumped to the different users and tanks on floors 30 and 57, from where the water is distributed according to demand by height.

Wastewater and rainwater are treated locally for reuse in the cooling towers and toilets on the lowest ten floors, as well as for irrigation of gardens, which reduces to zero the discharge of wastewaters to the city's drainage system.

The thermal protection incorporated into the design of the three façades minimizes solar gain. This reduces the demand for refrigerated water for the mechanical cooling system. The total demand of the building—1,508 RT—is met by three chillers rated at 433 RT each, and an additional 209 RT joker chiller to provide 24/7 service to

Prevailing winds

	Jan	Feb	Mar	Apr	May	Jun	Jul	Aug	Sep	Oct	Nov	Dec	**Whole year**	Winter	Summer
North	**42**	**58**	**40**	**27**	**53**	**24**	**79**	**76**	**57**	**60**	**48**	**50**	**51%**	**50%**	**53%**
North-east	12	9	7	10	12	16	4	10	15	10	9	8	10%	9%	11%
East	12	6	11	16	7	14	3	3	9	9	8	14	9%	10%	9%
South-east	13	7	12	10	5	11	3	2	3	7	15	9	8%	11%	6%
South	7	6	15	13	4	8	2	2	1	3	8	6	6%	8%	5%
South-west	2	2	6	8	4	6	1	1	1	2	2	2	3%	3%	4%
West	4	6	6	8	7	10	5	3	4	3	5	3	5%	5%	6%
North-west	7	7	3	9	8	10	2	3	10	7	4	8	7%	6%	7%

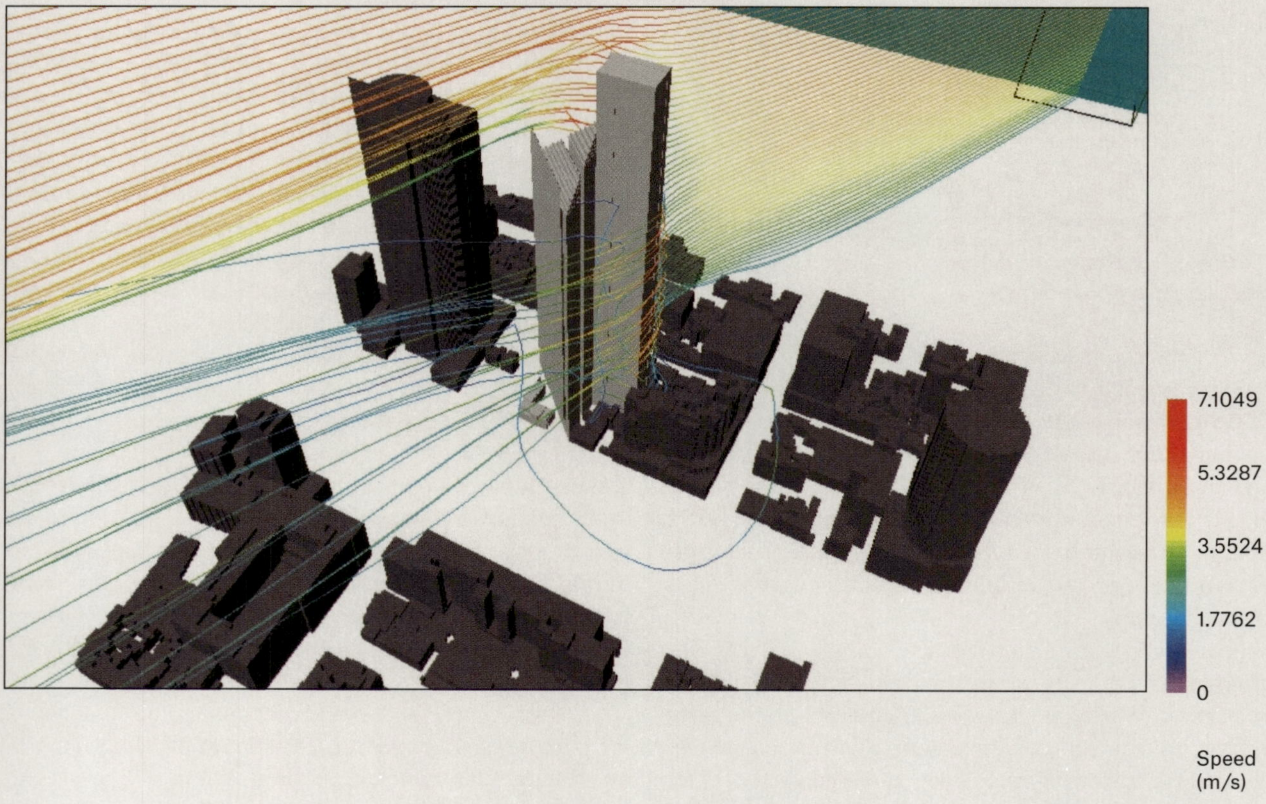

Annual temperature and insolation

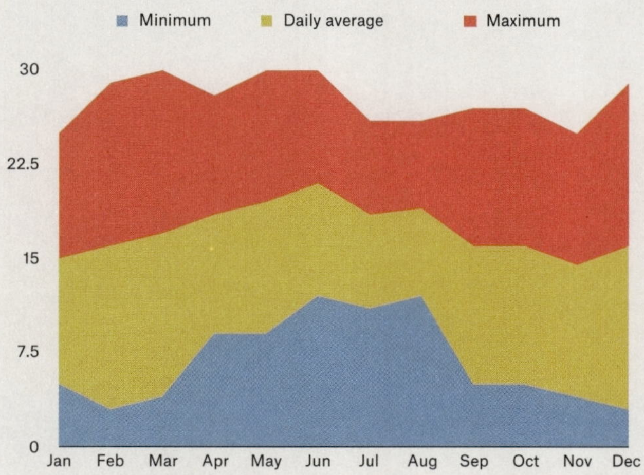

June 21

December 21

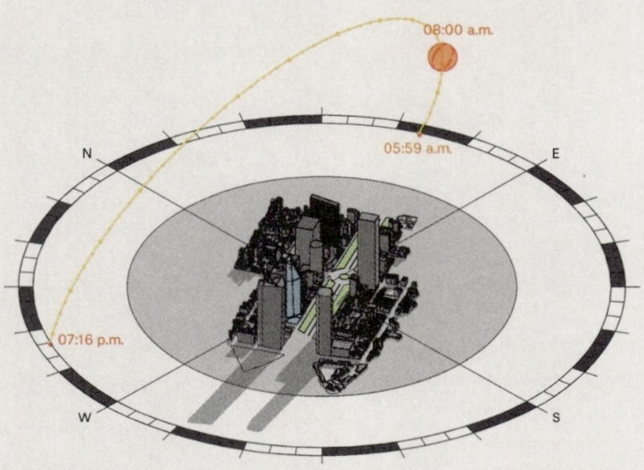

08:00 h

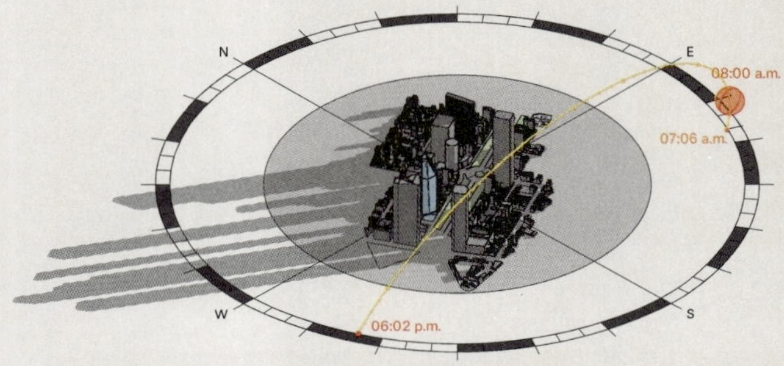

08:00 h

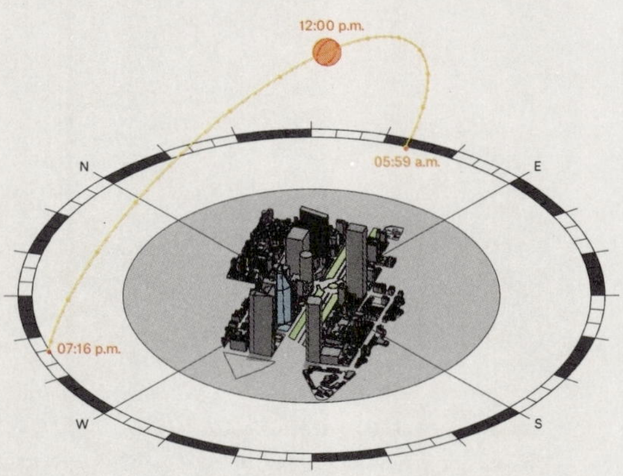

12:00 h

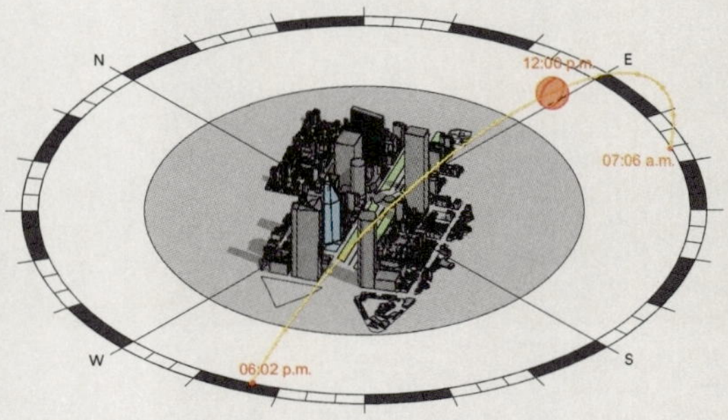

12:00 h

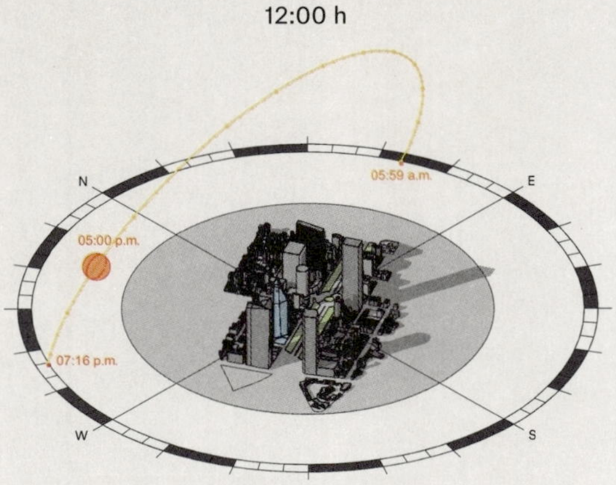

17:00 h

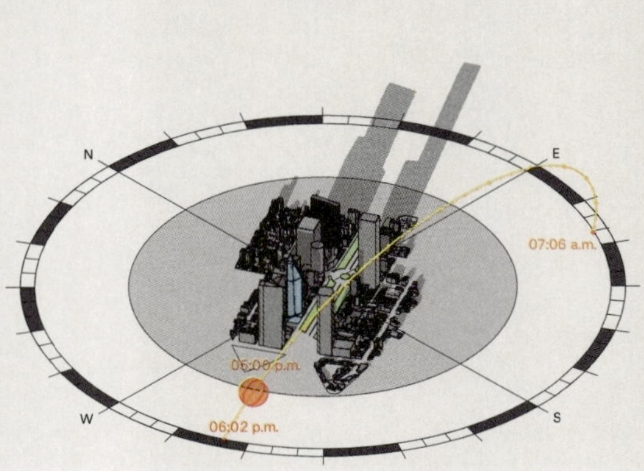

17:00 h

Solar protection studies

University of Pennsylvania

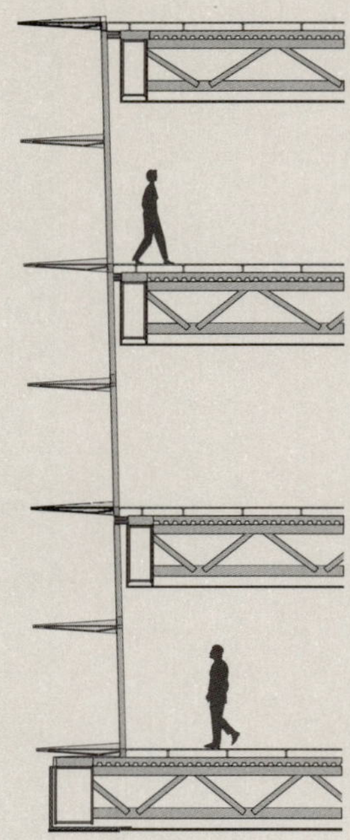

Torre Reforma

Solar gain study

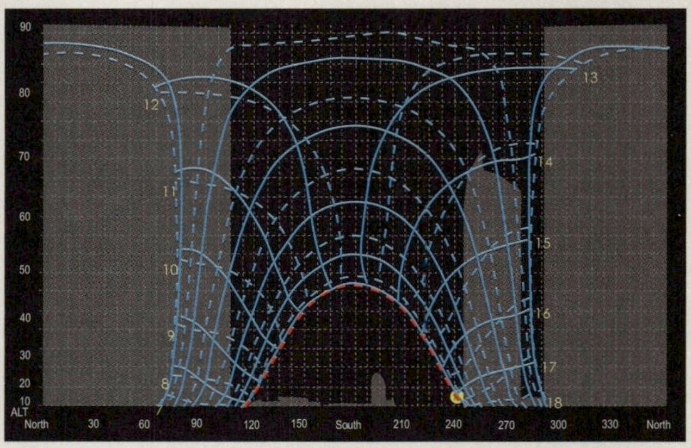

Point 3, December 21

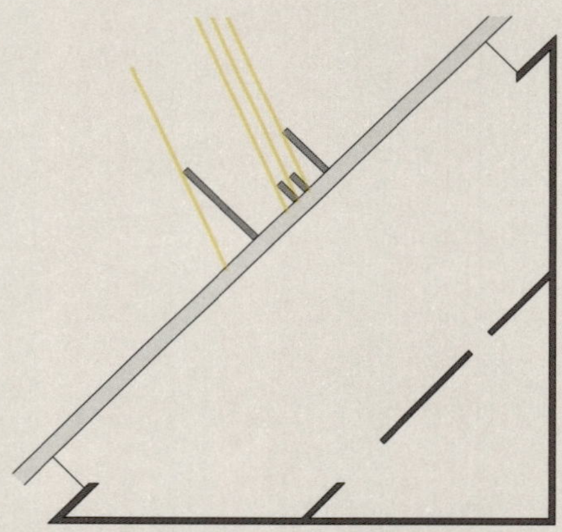

University of Pennsylvania

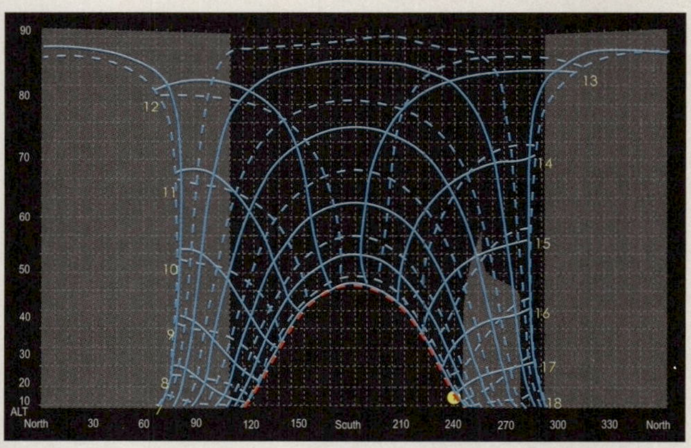

Point 2, August 21

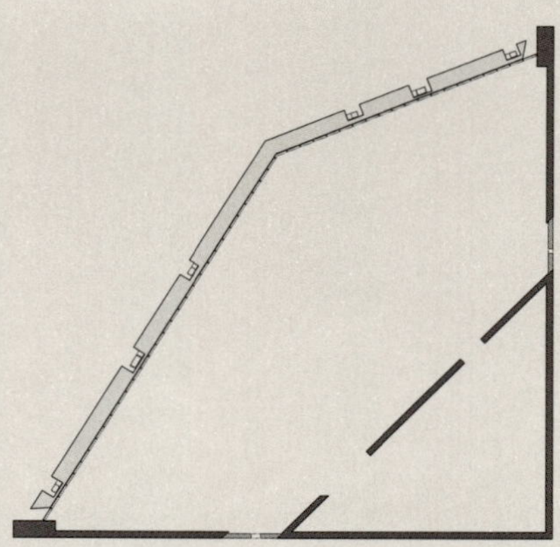

Torre Reforma

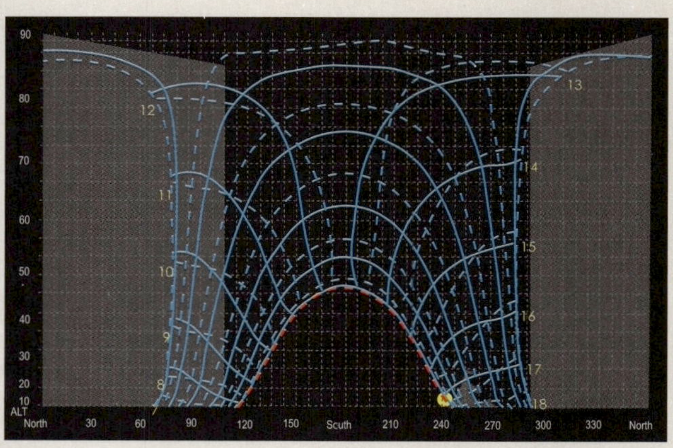

Point 1, August 21

Wind spectrum at different heights

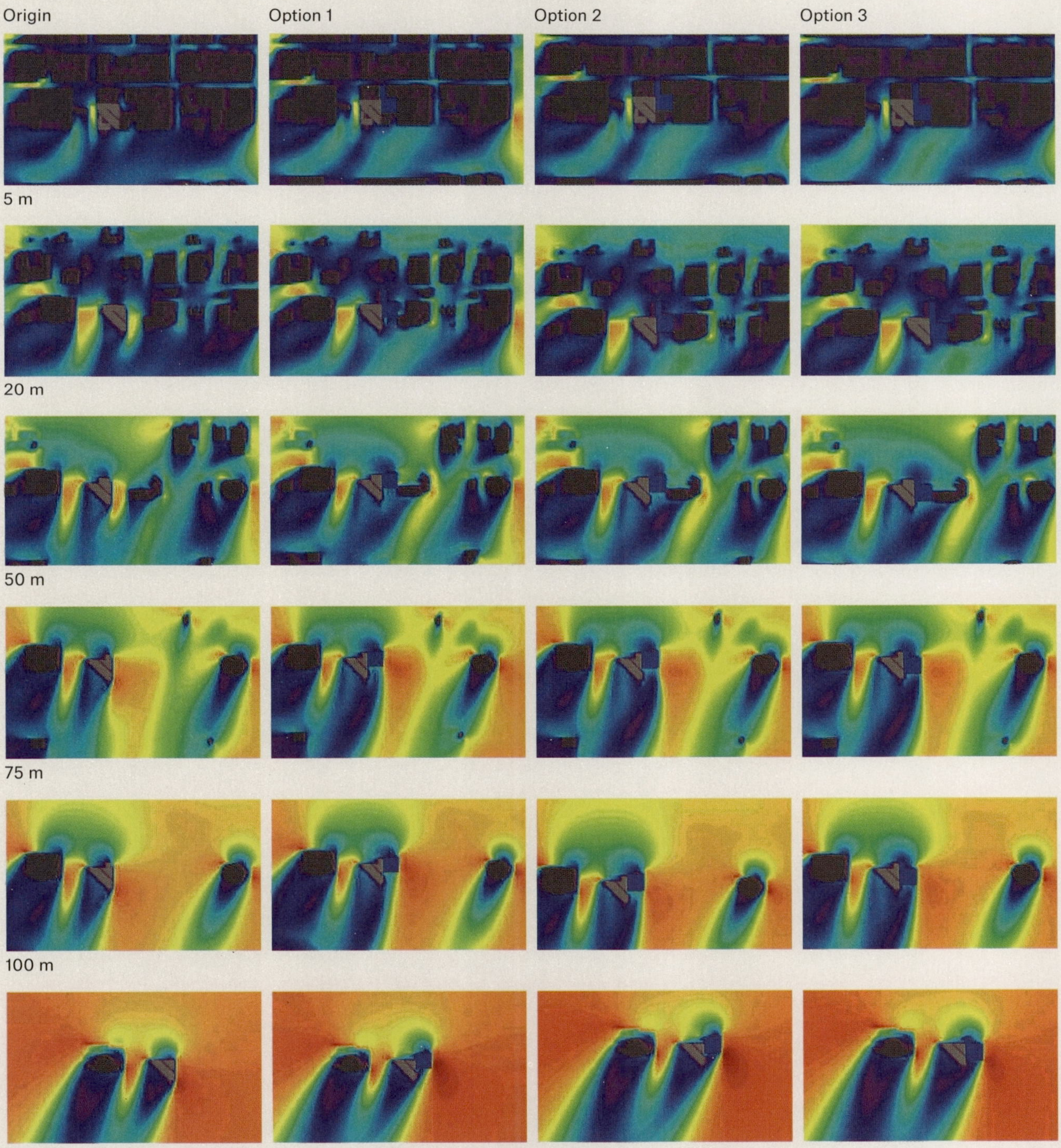

occupants for their IT systems. The design also contemplates the efficient use of space, with a strong understanding of the climate's impact and the comfort of inhabitants, significantly reducing energy consumption by 25.4% by comparison with similar buildings in Mexico City. As a result, Torre Reforma was awarded Platinum LEED certification in 2016.

To understand the operation of the building in three dimensions and the interaction of the different flows, we used the Building Information Modeling (BIM) computer system. The BIM begins by defining the geometry in three dimensions and then inserts the various engineering systems. Without it, it would have been impossible to visualize the correct functioning of the geometry and flows, as well as the clashes between the elements, such as between the structural metalwork and the masonry fittings. Each week we had BIM sessions where we all got together—just like the classes I teach at the Iberoamericana University—to work on the clashes between the different installations identified by this system. The meetings were always led by Miguel Rodríguez and Luis Manuel Sánchez, together with our team—César Balmes, Harón Kababie and myself—and we coordinated with the workshop led by Julieta the corrections to be made together with those responsible for each type of engineering. Sometimes we laughed when we realized how clumsy the flows can become if they are designed separately in two dimensions. We see this as a vital tool for the correct design of engineering systems in architectural spaces.

With regard to vehicle parking, due to a bizarre building code in force in the capital, a total of 1,100 parking spaces had to be incorporated, which undermines the efficient flow of users entering and exiting. The accesses to the basement parking floors are on two different streets, with permanent entrance and exit ramps and a two-way ramp that is used in alternating modes at peak times. In addition, a robotic parking system was installed including four redundant sets of equipment and independent entrances and exits.

The flow of pedestrians enters the building from two different streets, while services and waste management use a third street. The tower is divided into four blocks of different spaces: retail and sports facilities; the lower clusters of offices and the mid- and high-rise clusters of

Visuals generated using *Building Information Modeling* (BIM)

Review of the BIM model

offices. Users of the high and mid-rise floors reach the sky lobby on floor 23 with express elevators, while users of the low-rise floors take elevators on the first floor. The sports facilities and retail area use different street entrances to the elevator hub.

Given the building's height, and in response to the exit study, two pressurized emergency staircases were installed, together with a fire shelter beside the elevators on each floor. These are designed to activate in the event of a fire. The emergency staircases, the fire shelter, the elevator shafts, public toilets and MEP vertical ducts share the same vertical column throughout the building—they are the core defined by the architectural partition. The blocks of high-, mid- and low-rise elevators, public toilets and MEP cabinets change location by block, which increases the energy efficiency of the 29 elevators in the building. The high-rise and shuttle elevators are the only ones with high-speed equipment in the building, which reduces total energy consumption by elevators by 281.9 kW.

The construction process for the tower can be read as an intrinsic part of the project's façade, which responds to the process of pouring the concrete, the views, the mechanical and the ventilation openings, as well as the cracks that may be generated in the concrete by the tensions arising from seismic movements. The conception of the space and the structure, the construction process and the complexity of the project, given the small footprint of the building, are visible both on the exterior and the interior, in a harmonious volumetric coexistence that reveals that architecture is at once structure and energy behavior.

The human desire to live in cities inevitably increases the use of the skyscraper typology. Skyscraper designers have been obsessed with the image of the buildings as glass prisms and have paid little attention to the behavior of energy and of flows. This impacts on the energy and structural efficiency of the constructions, as well as the human comfort and quality of the interior and exterior spaces, with the consequence that both the initial construction cost and the ongoing maintenance costs of the building rise.

A proper understanding of the architectural parti, based on flows, form, context and structural integration, together with a correct interpretation of vernacular architecture, can help to achieve the objective that the American Institute of Architecture (AIA) has for the year 2030: to achieve a carbon-free footprint through the design of net zero-energy buildings.

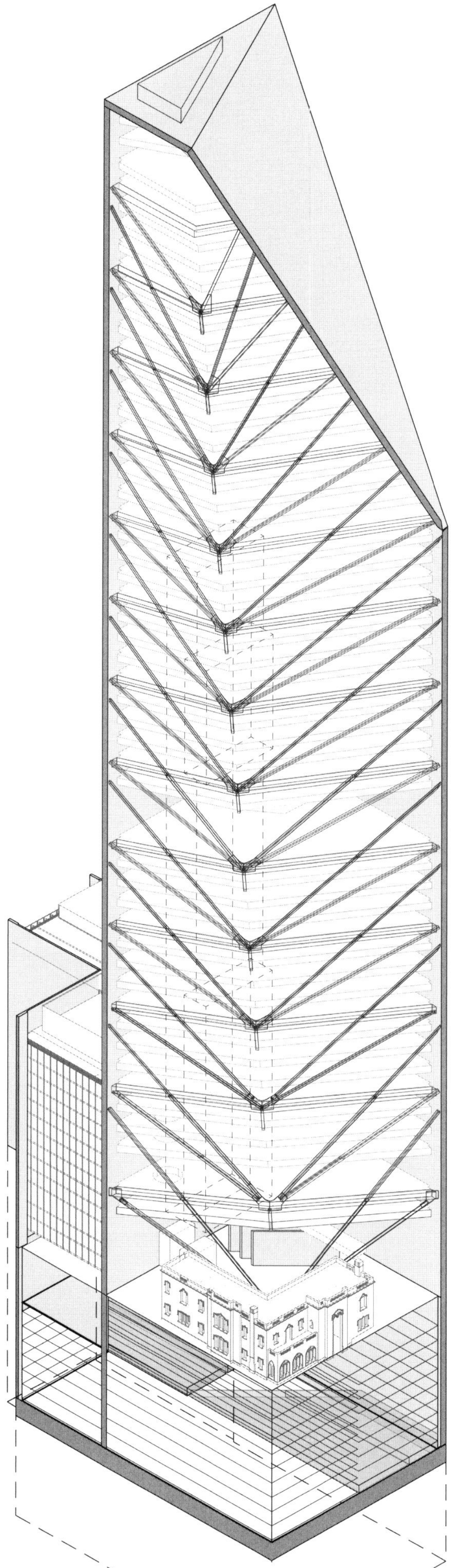

059

FIRE PROTECTION FLOW

Section

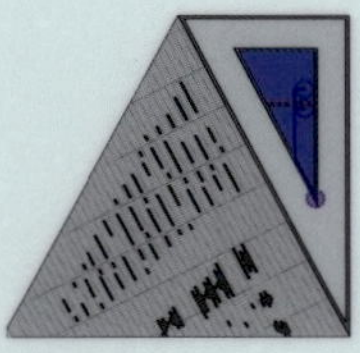

Rooftop

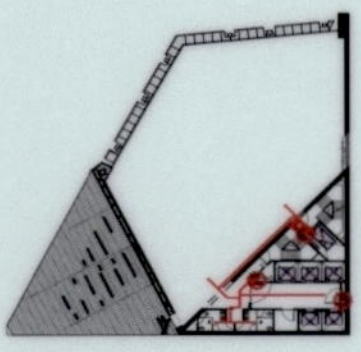

Level 47

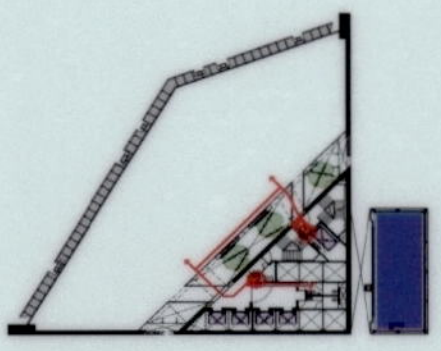

Level 30

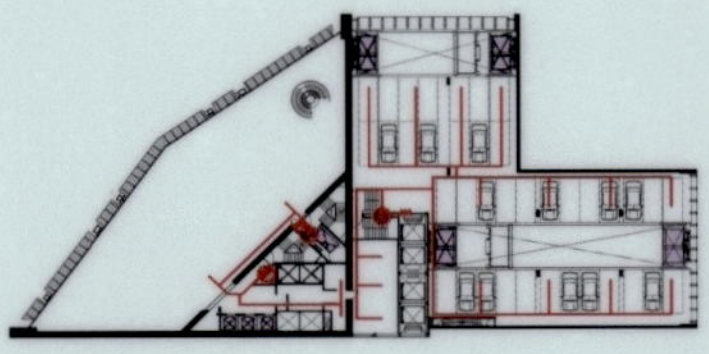

Level 7

Standard basement floorplan

FIRE PROTECTION FLOW

Section

Rooftop

Level 47

Level 30

Level 7

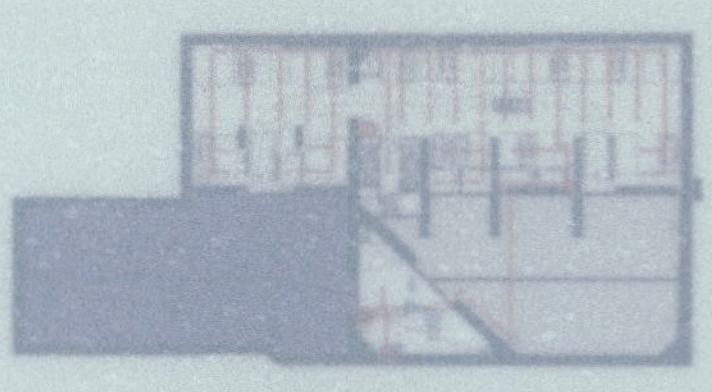

Standard basement floorplan

PLANS

0 15m

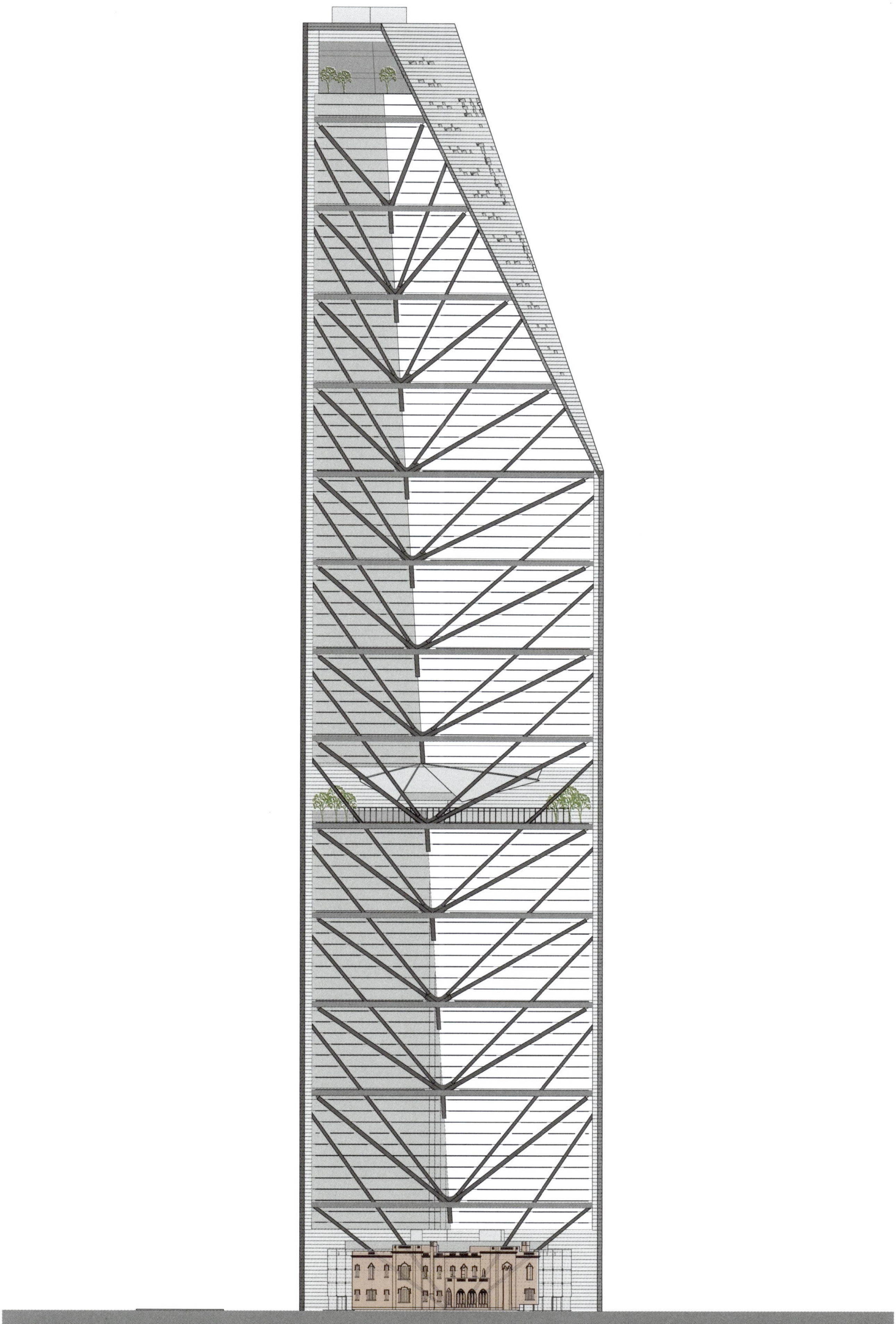

SOUTH FAÇADE

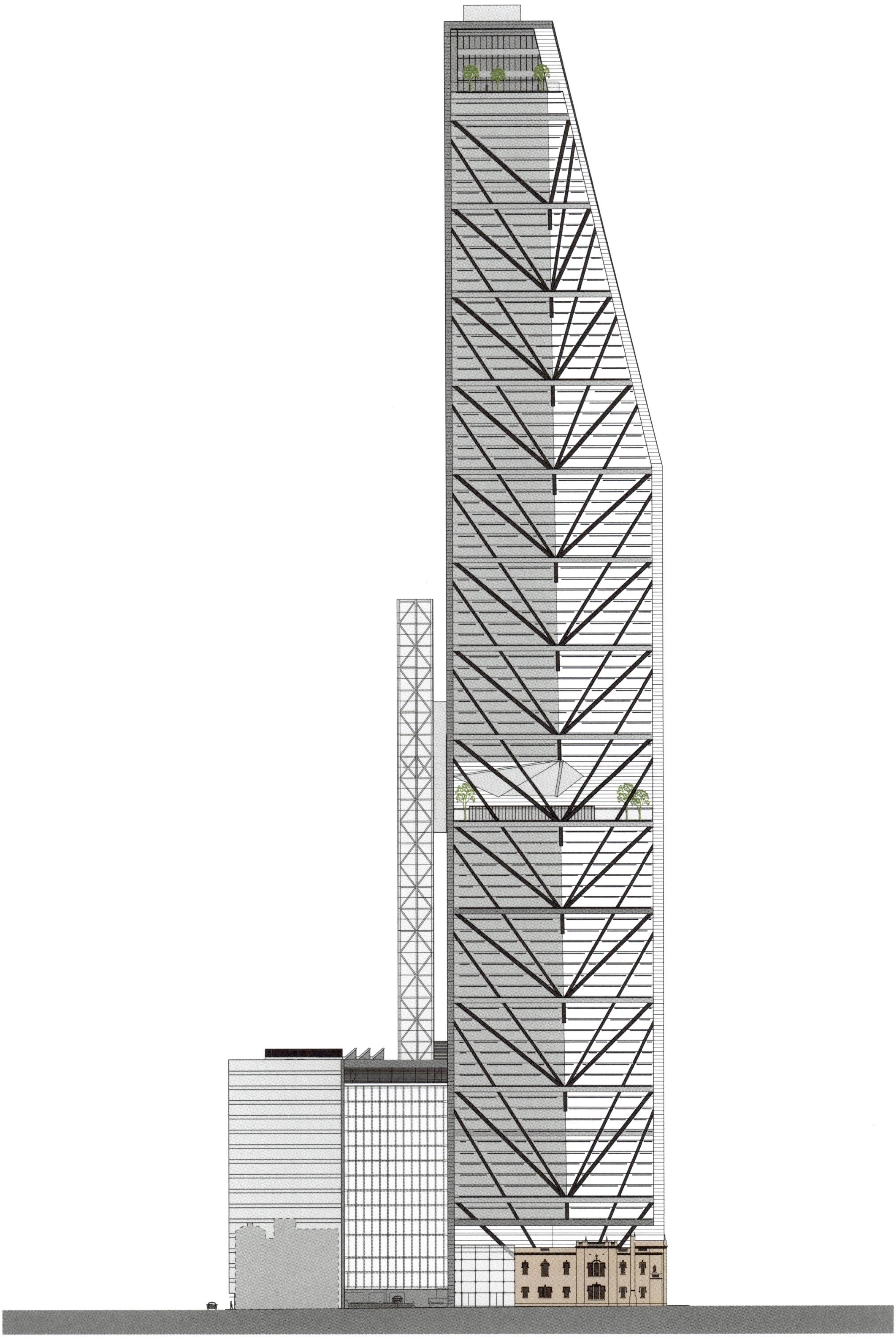

SOUTHWEST FAÇADE

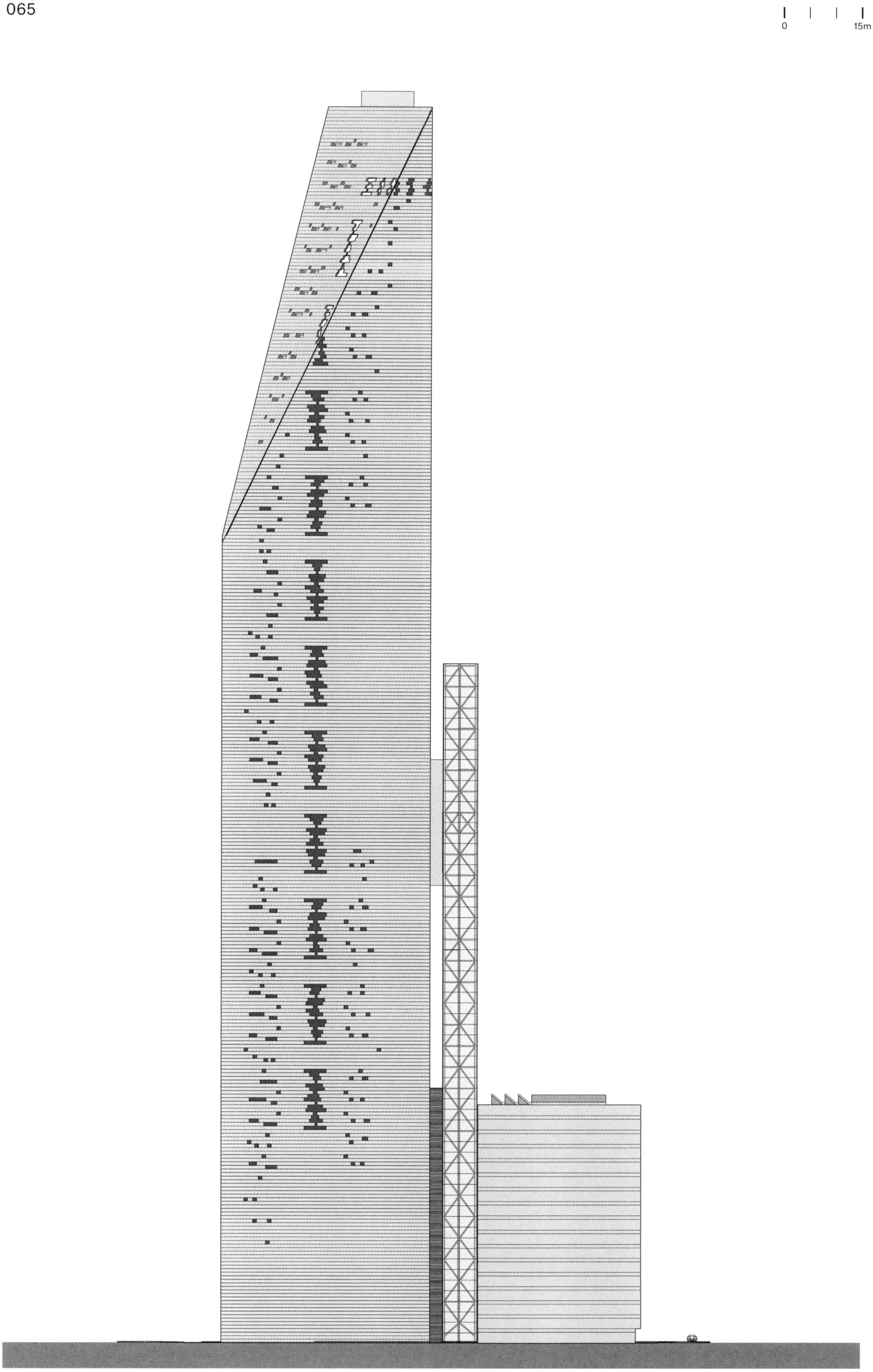

EAST FAÇADE

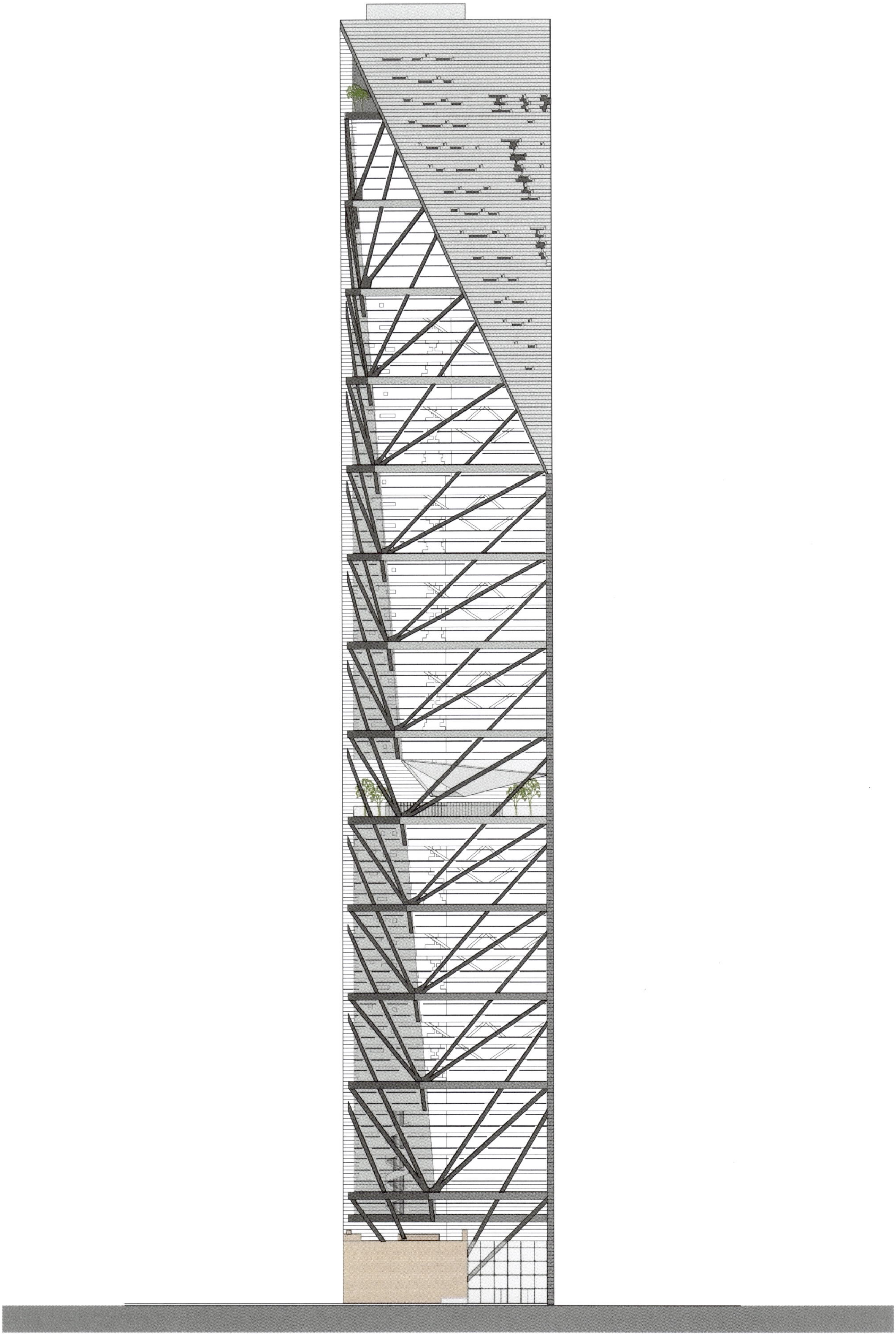

SOUTHEAST FAÇADE

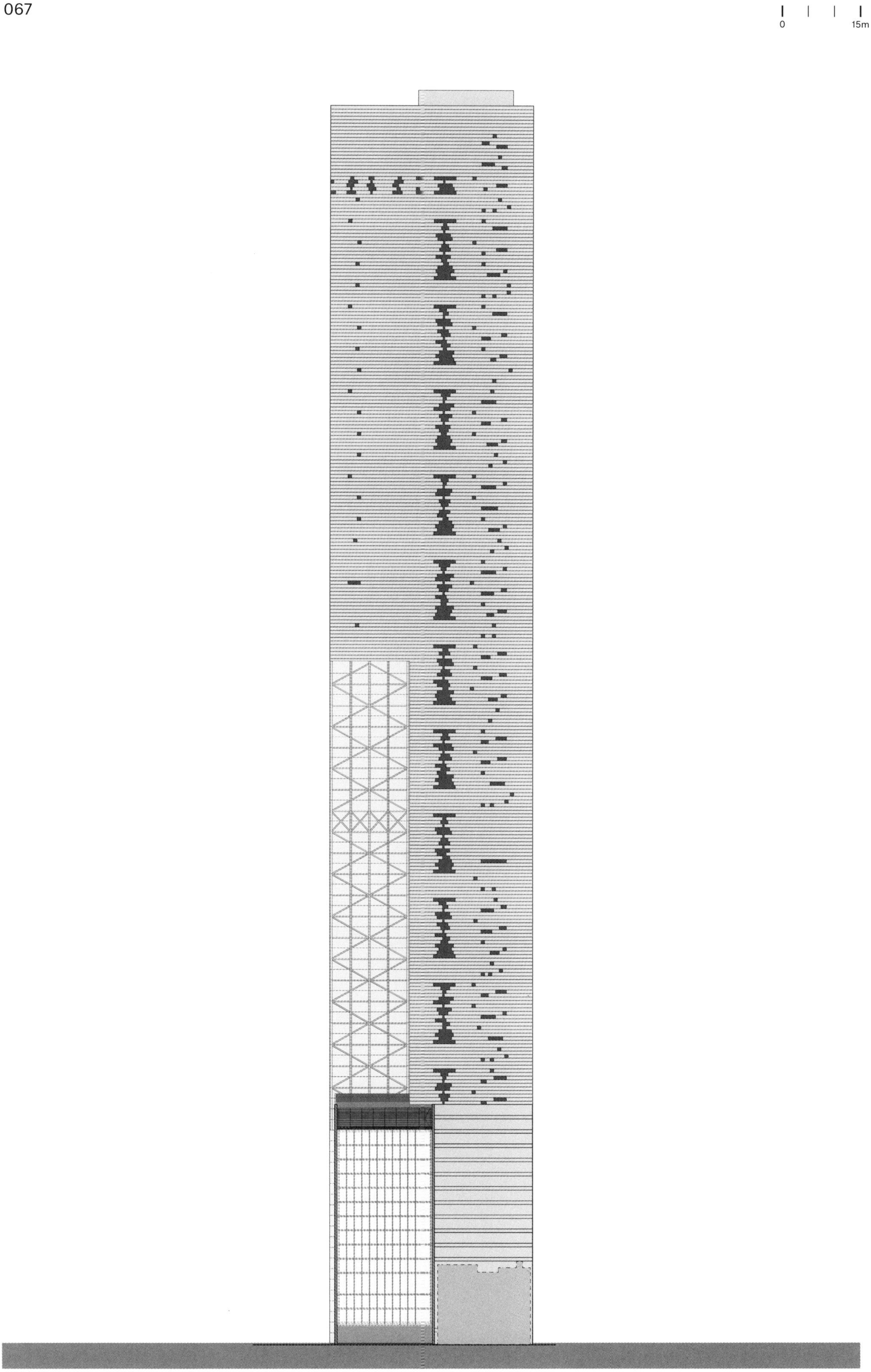

NORTH FAÇADE

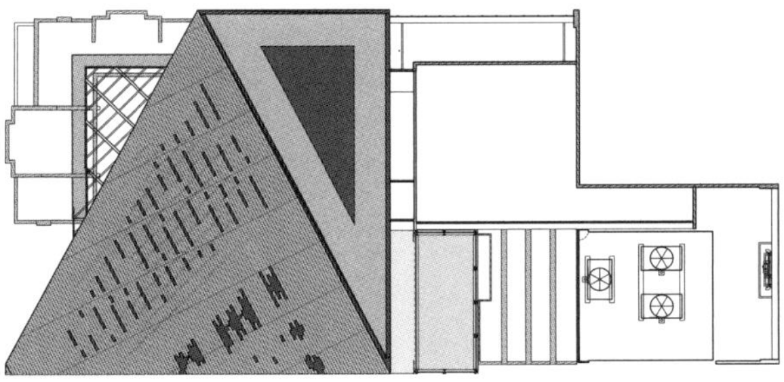

GENERAL PLAN

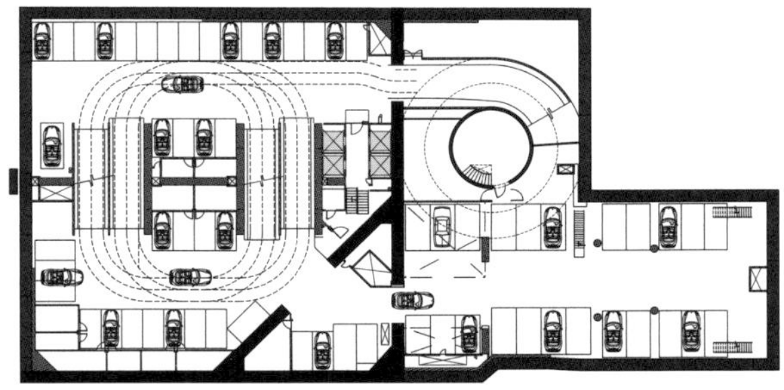

LEVEL -3

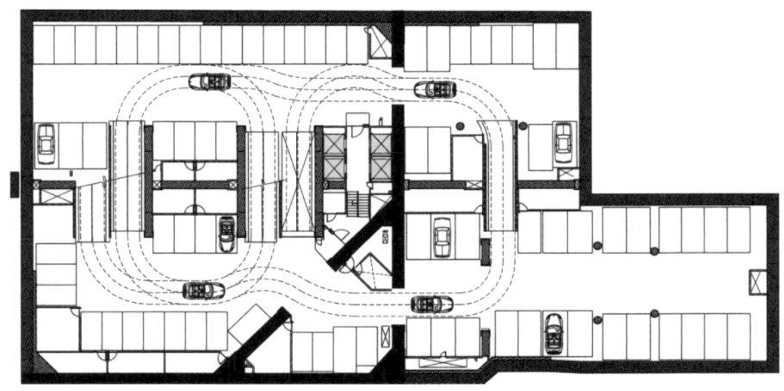

LEVEL -4

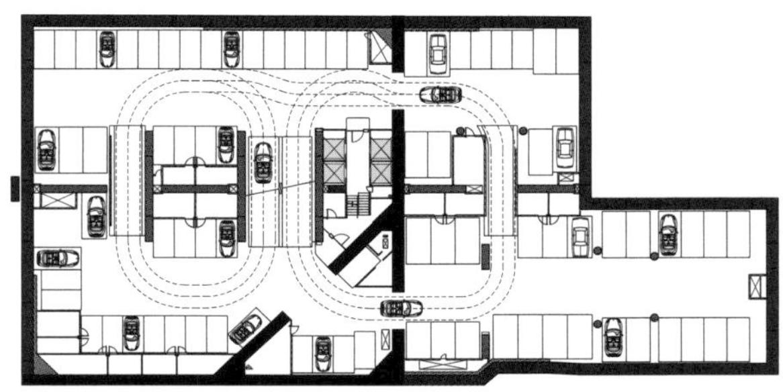

TYPICAL BASEMENT (LEVEL -8, -7, -6, -5)

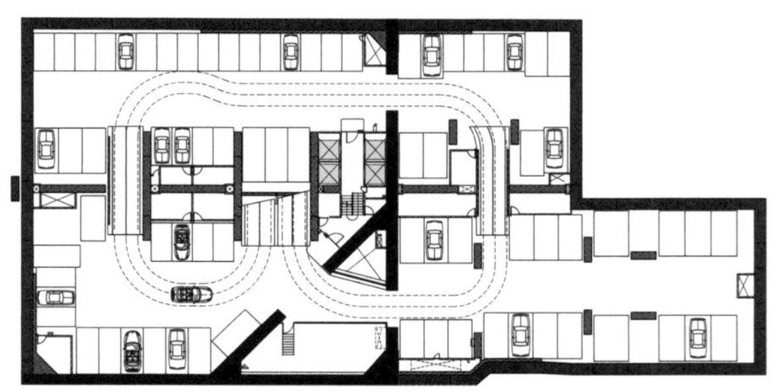

LEVEL -9

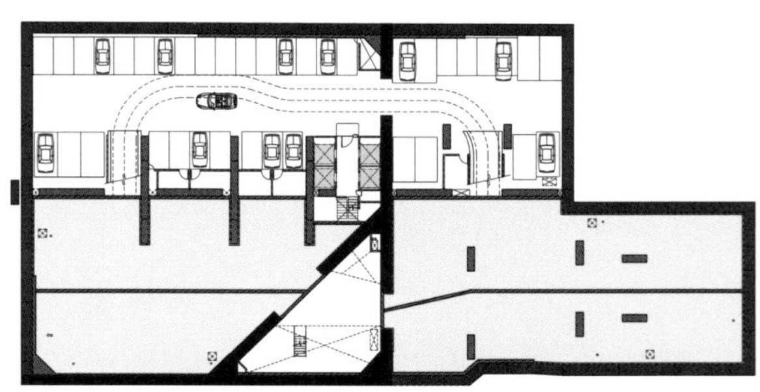

LEVEL -10

0 15m

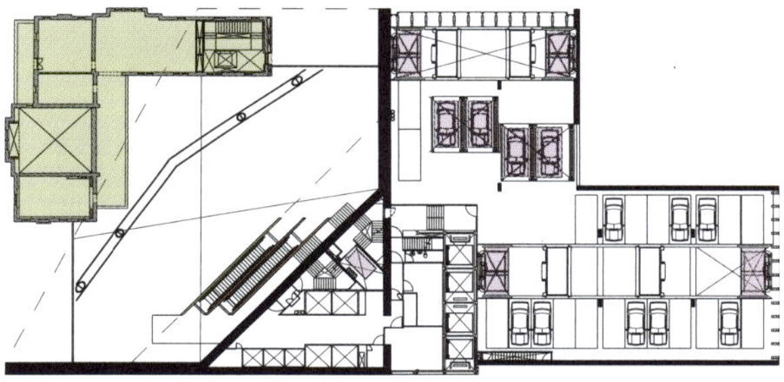

LEVEL 2

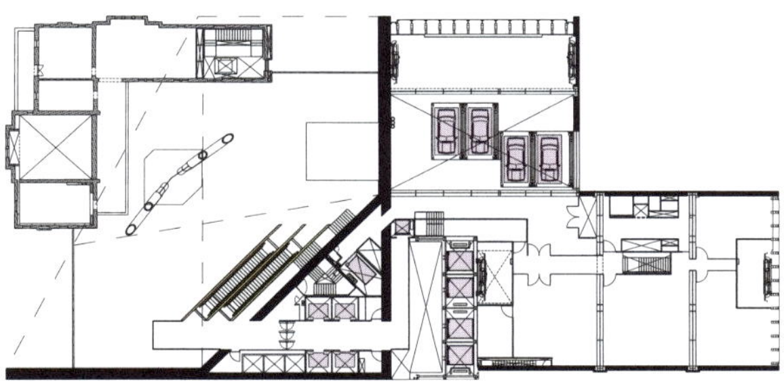

LEVEL 1

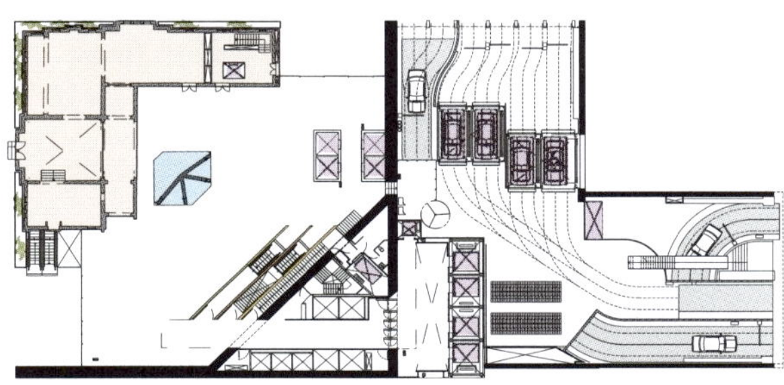

GROUND FLOOR

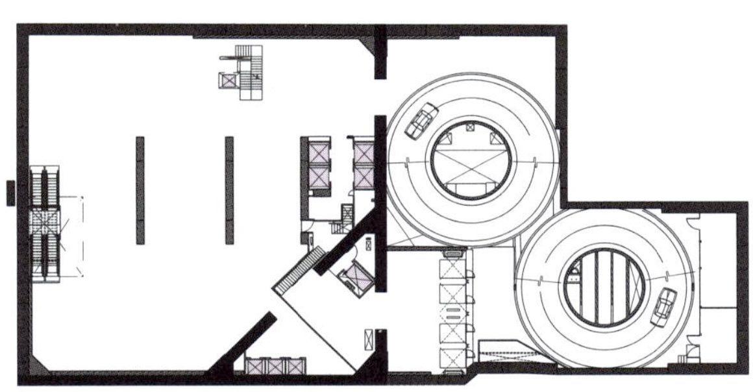

LEVEL -1

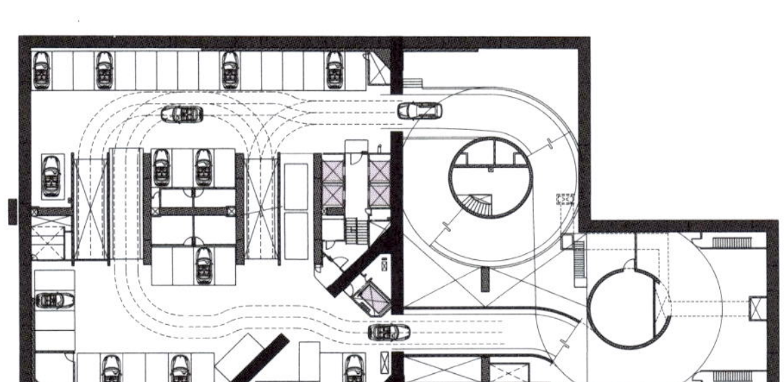

LEVEL -2

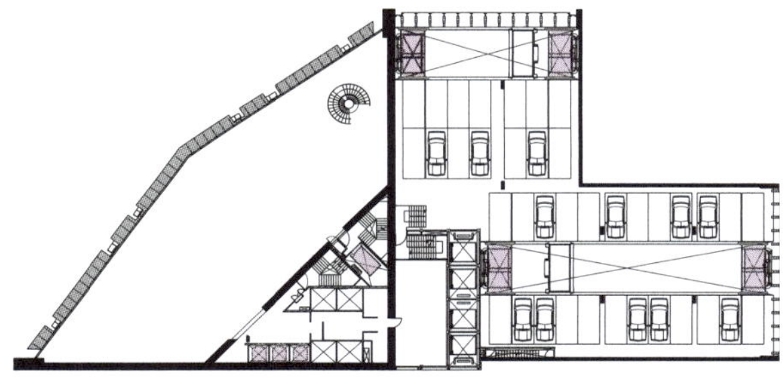

LEVEL 7

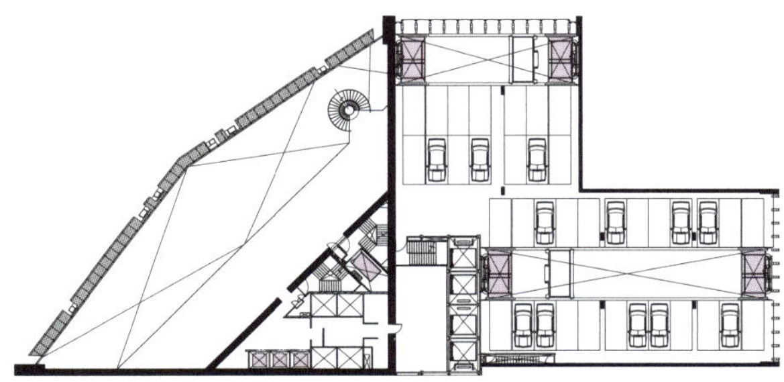

LEVEL 6

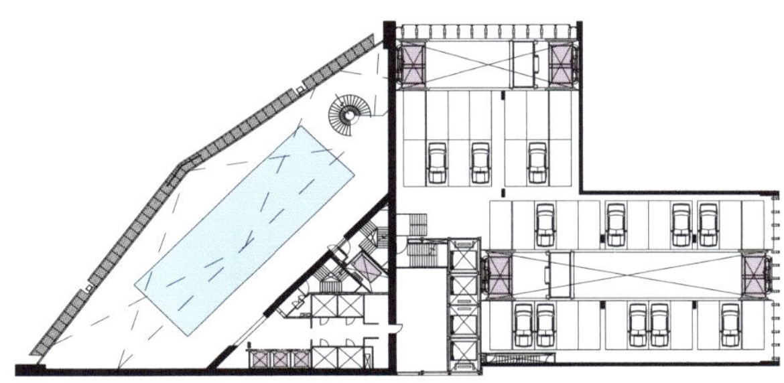

LEVEL 5

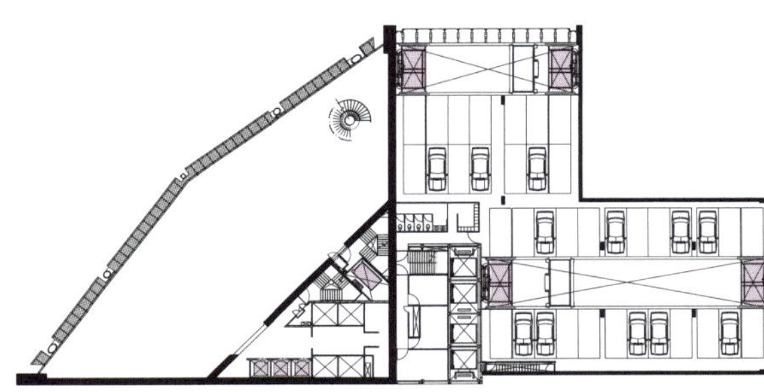

LEVEL 4

LEVEL 3

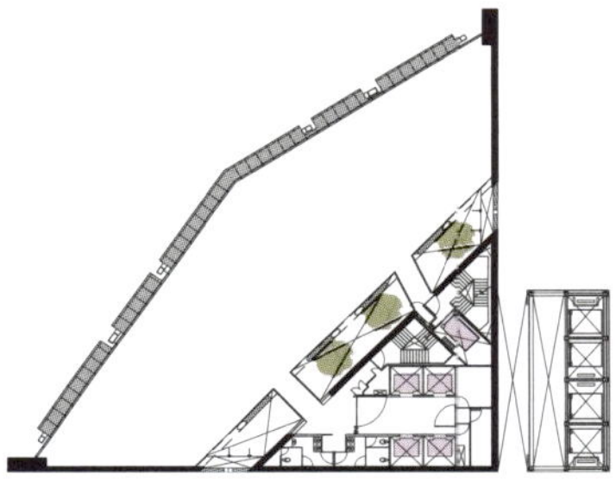

LEVEL 12

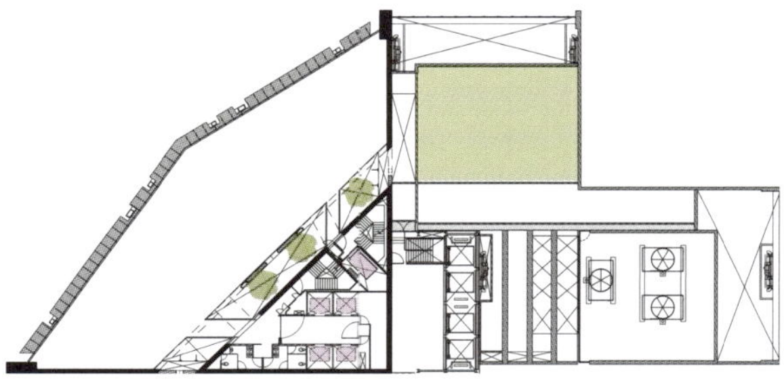

LEVEL 11

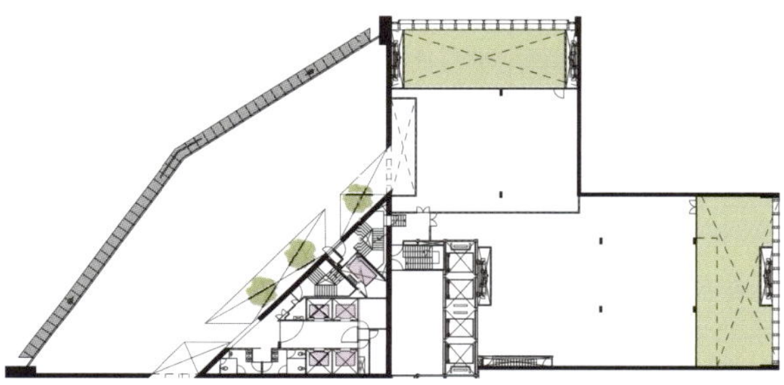

LEVEL 10

LEVEL 9

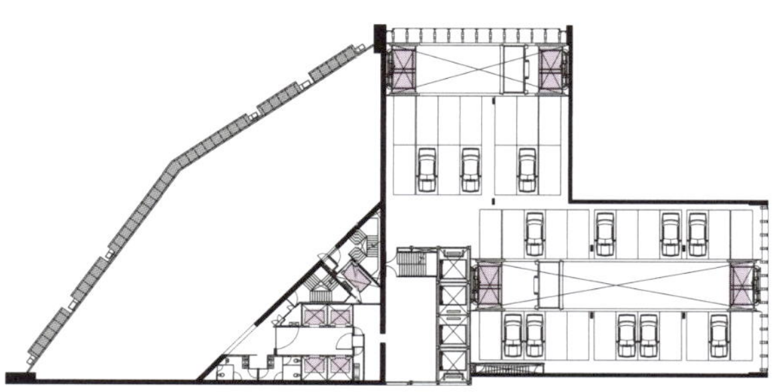

LEVEL 8

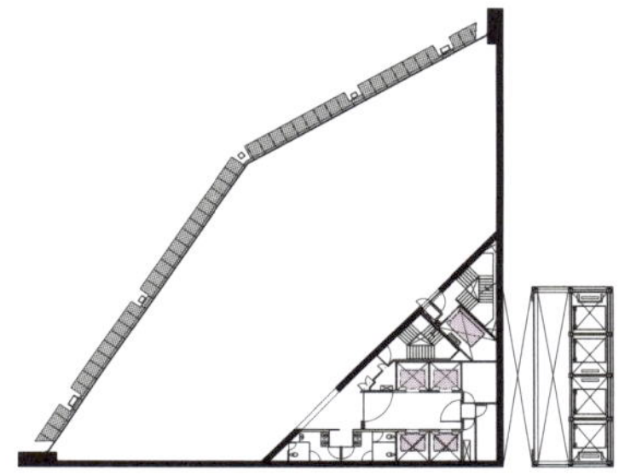

LEVEL 17

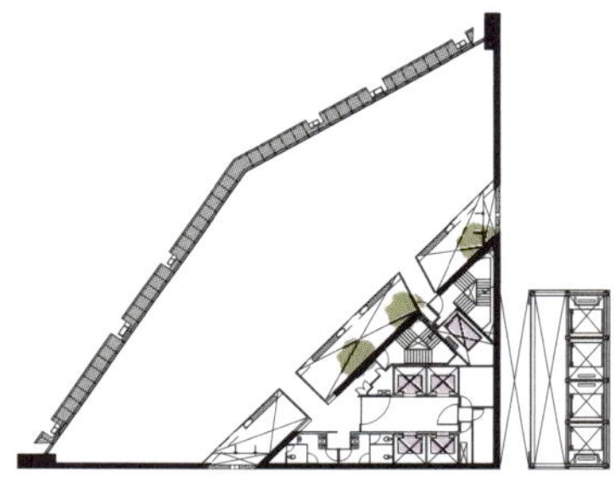

LEVEL 16

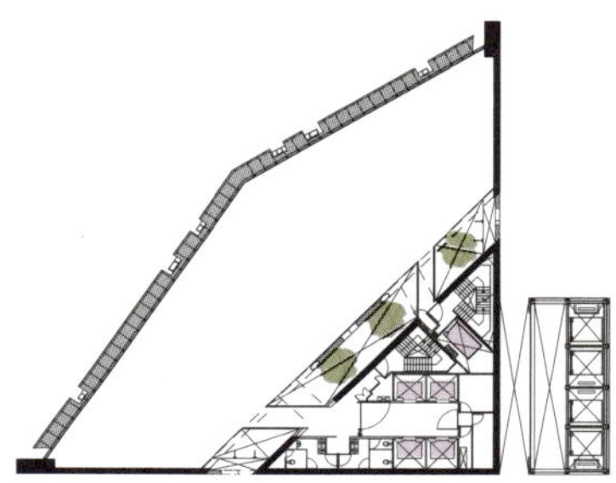

LEVEL 15

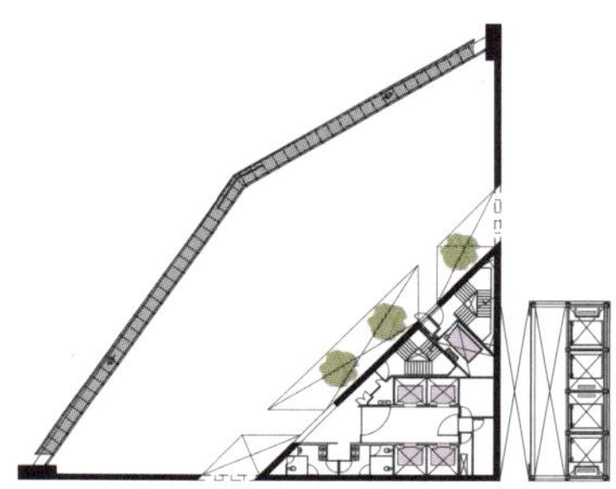

LEVEL 14

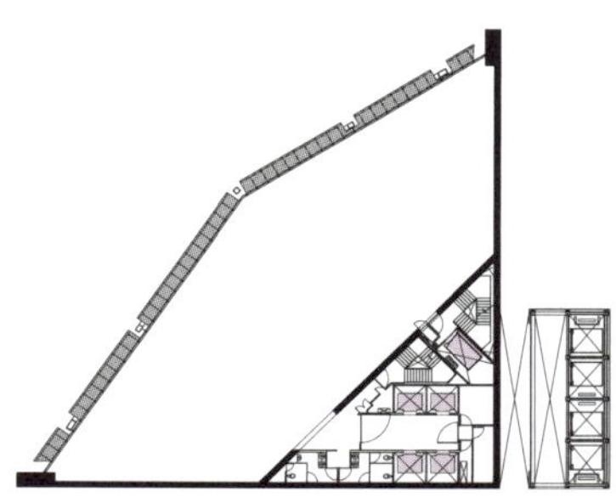

LEVEL 13

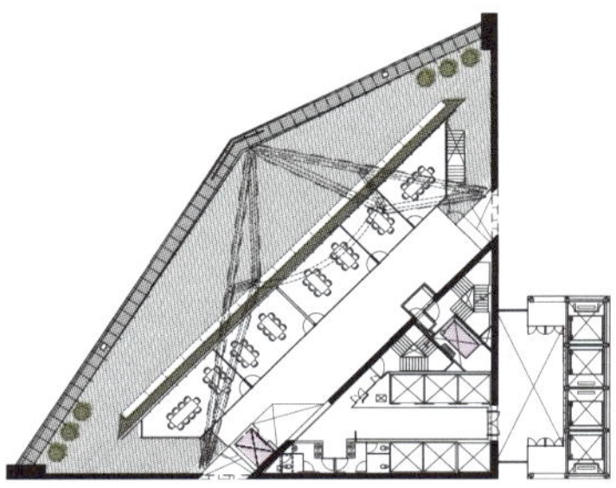

LEVEL 22 - Sky lobby

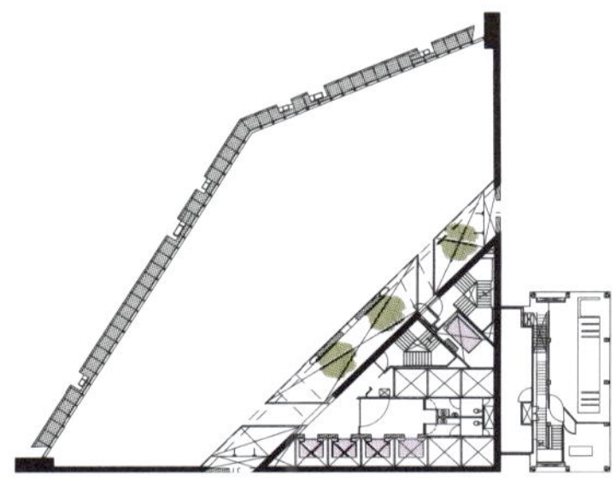

LEVEL 26

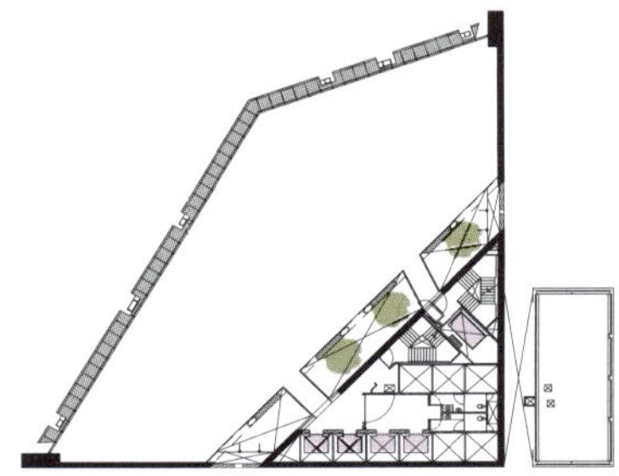

LEVEL 31

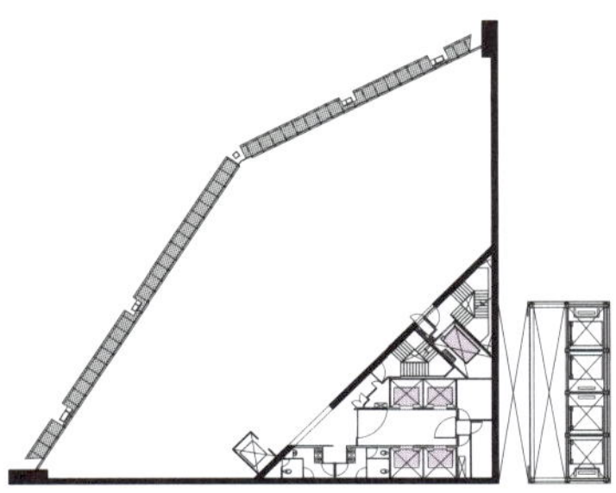

LEVEL 21

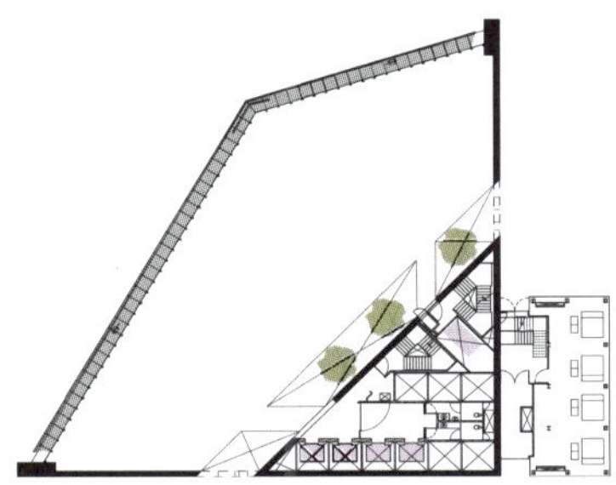

LEVEL 25

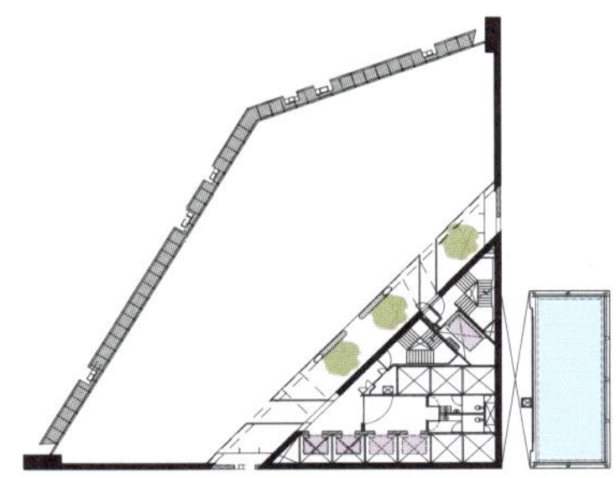

LEVEL 30

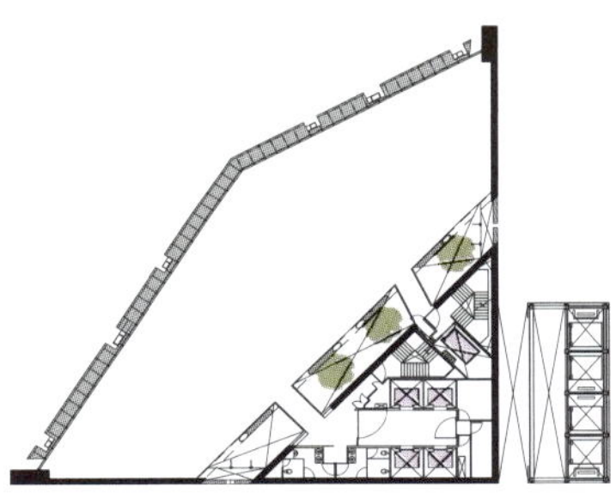

LEVEL 20

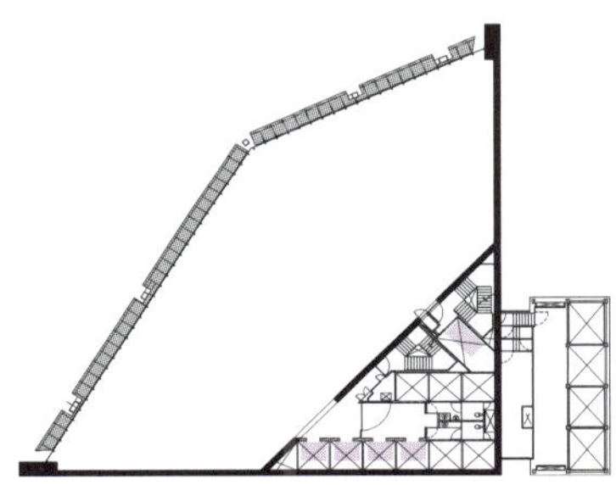

LEVEL 24

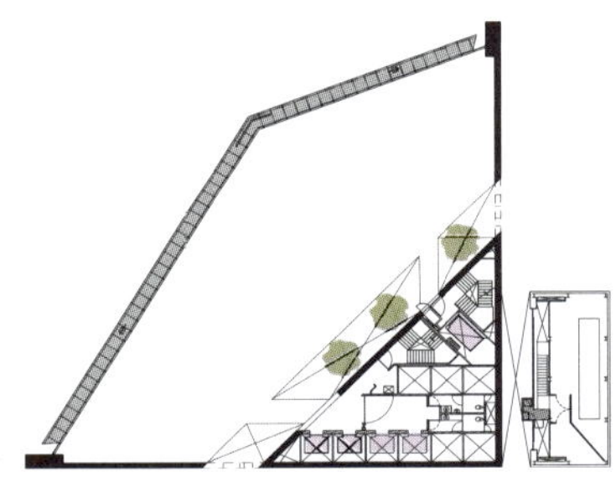

LEVEL 29

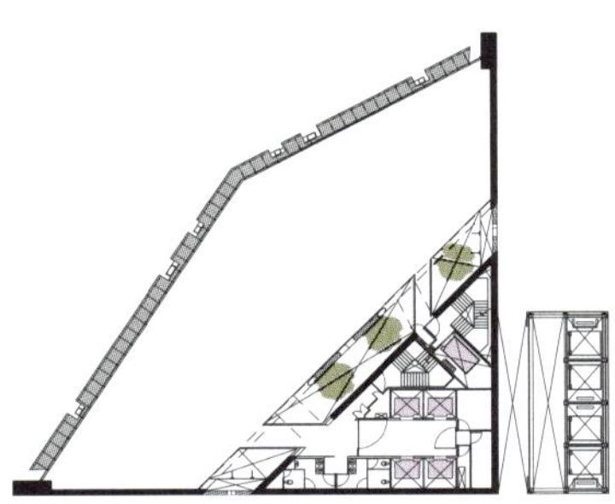

LEVEL 19

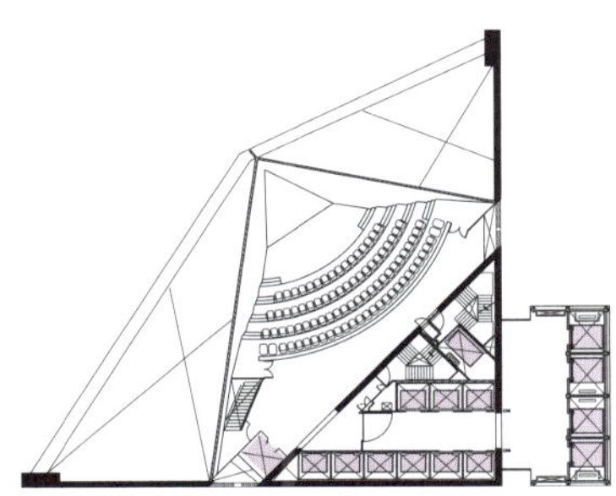

LEVEL 23 - Auditorium

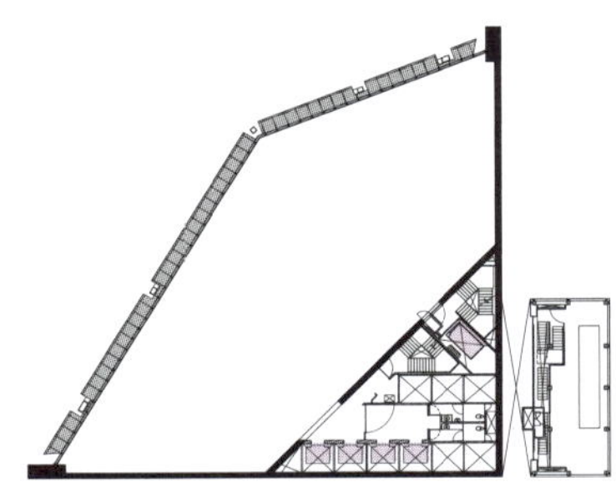

LEVEL 28

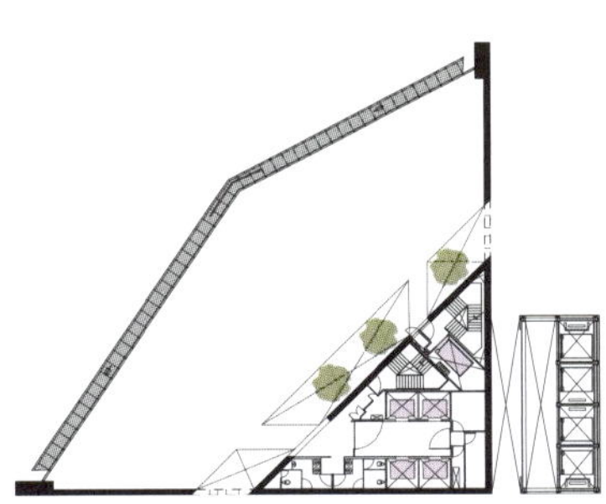

LEVEL 18

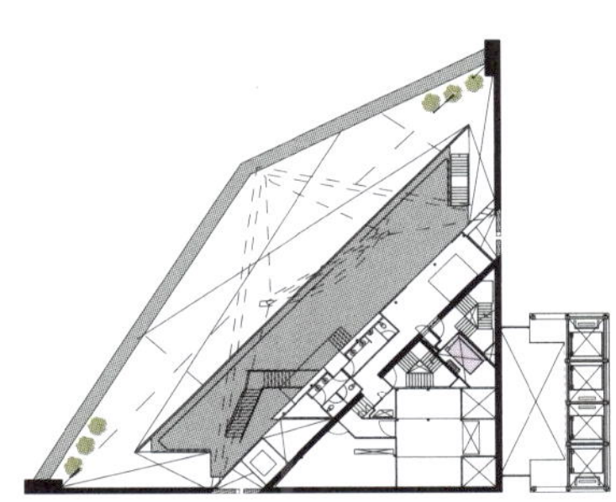

LEVEL 22A

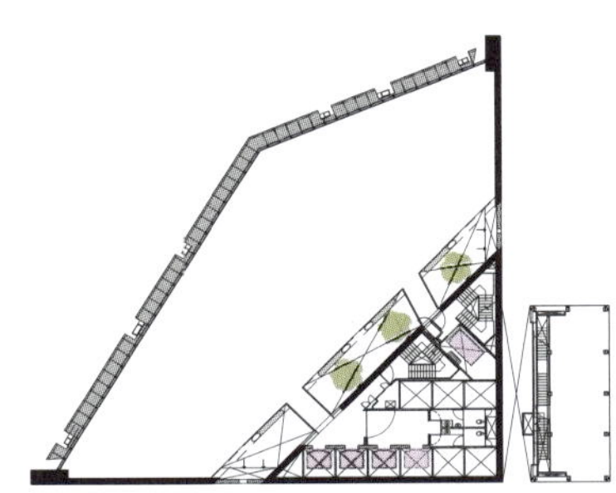

LEVEL 27

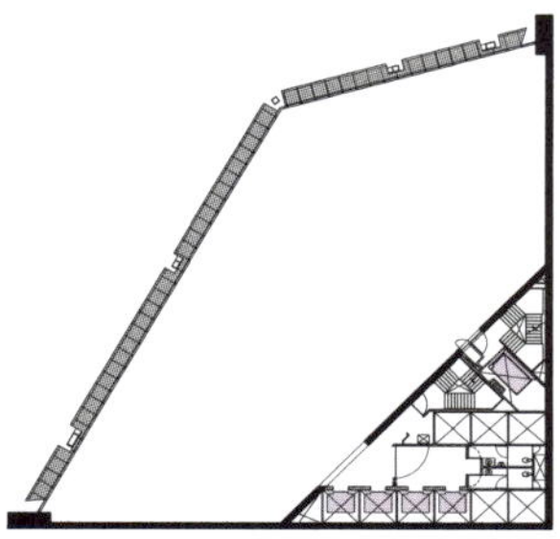

LEVEL 36

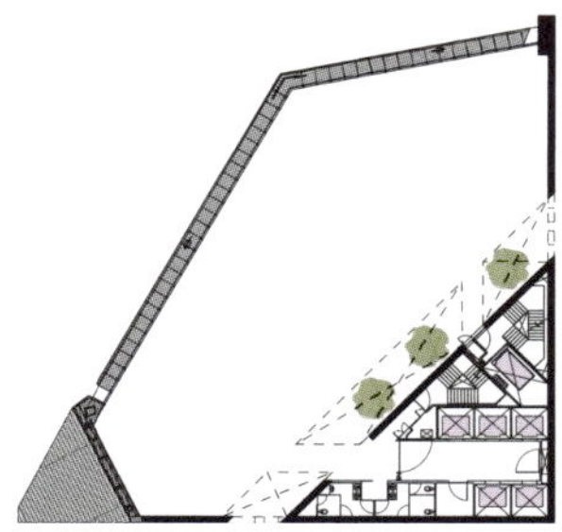

LEVEL 41

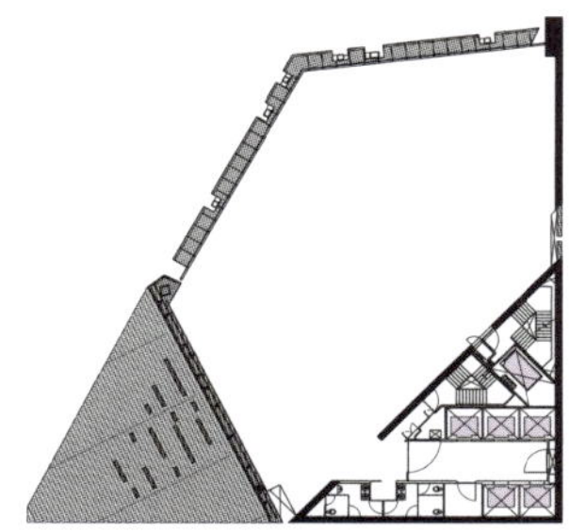

LEVEL 46

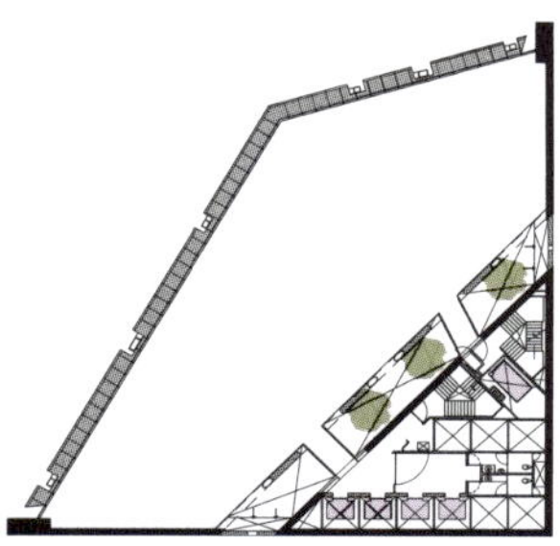

LEVEL 35

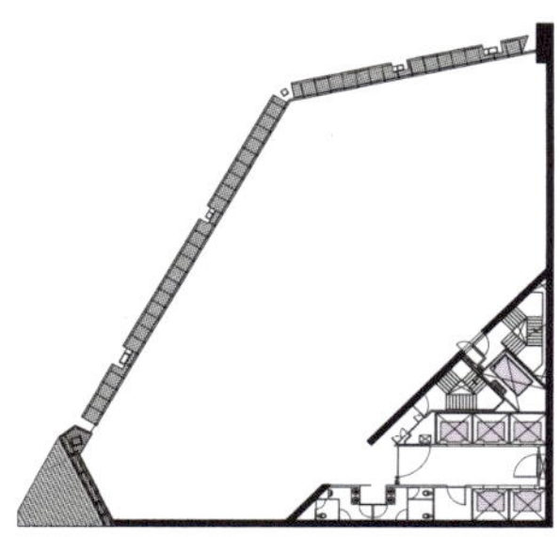

LEVEL 40

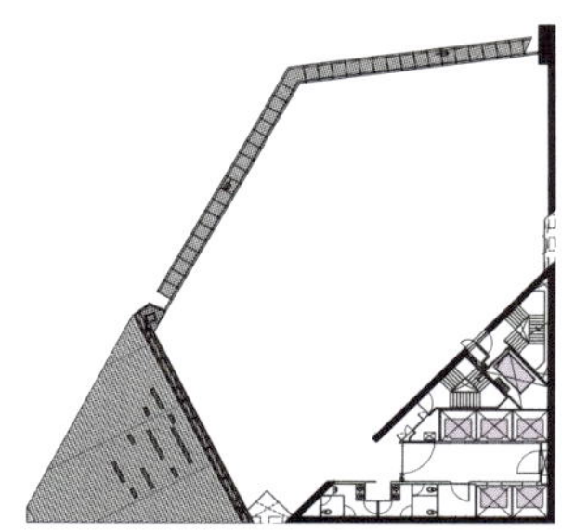

LEVEL 45

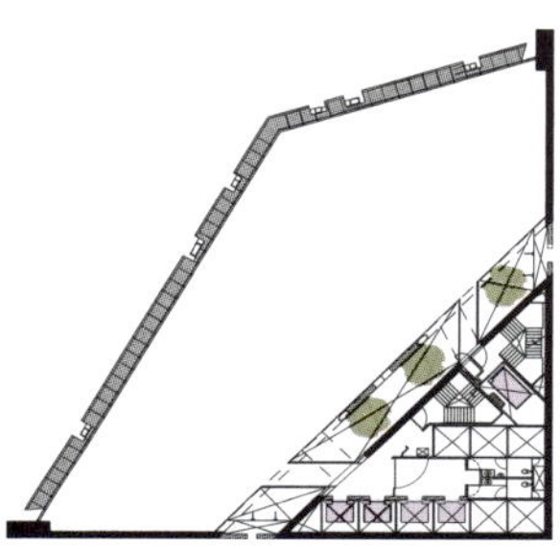

LEVEL 34

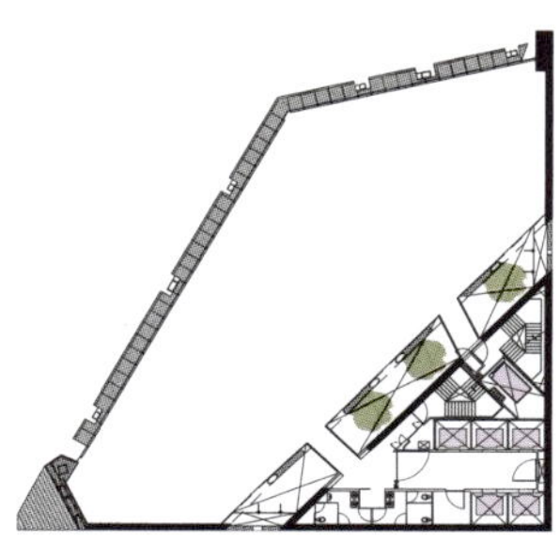

LEVEL 39

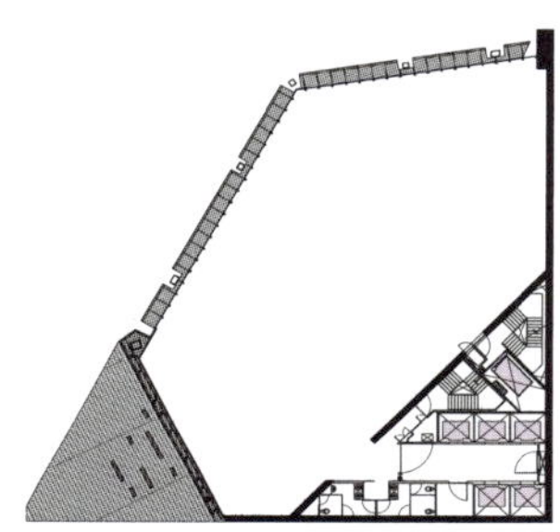

LEVEL 44

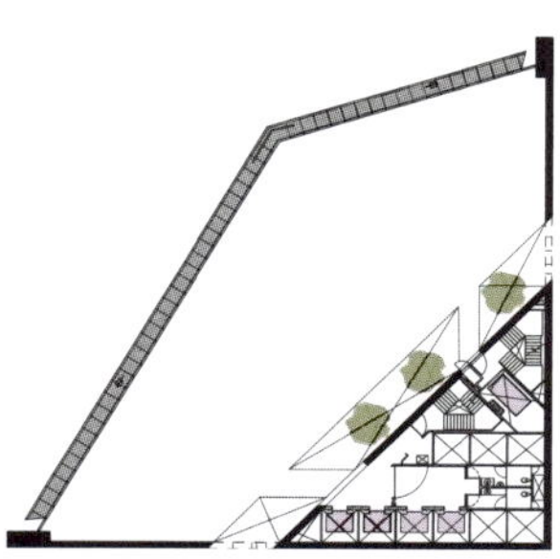

LEVEL 33

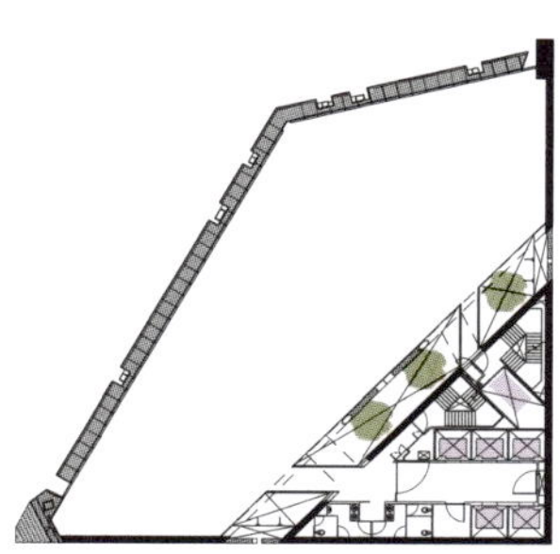

LEVEL 38

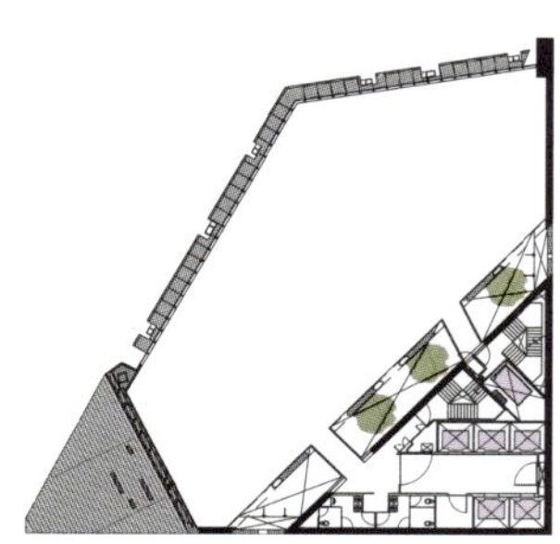

LEVEL 43

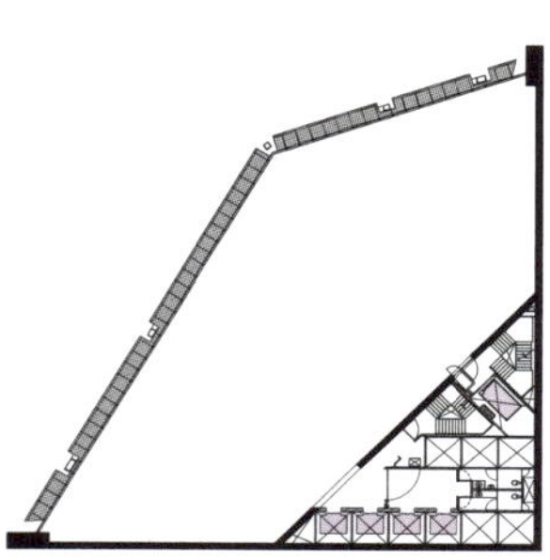

LEVEL 32

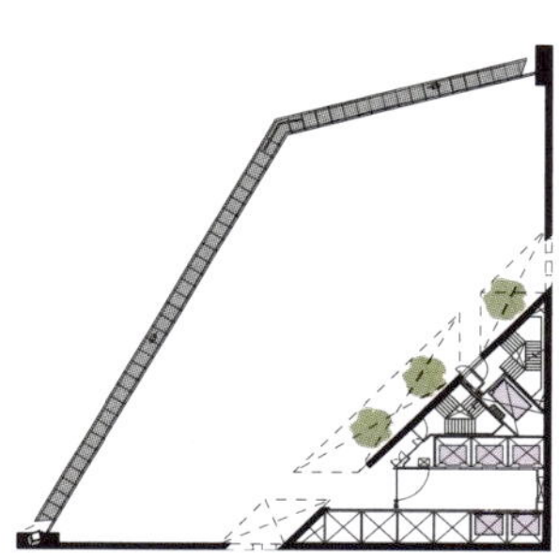

LEVEL 37

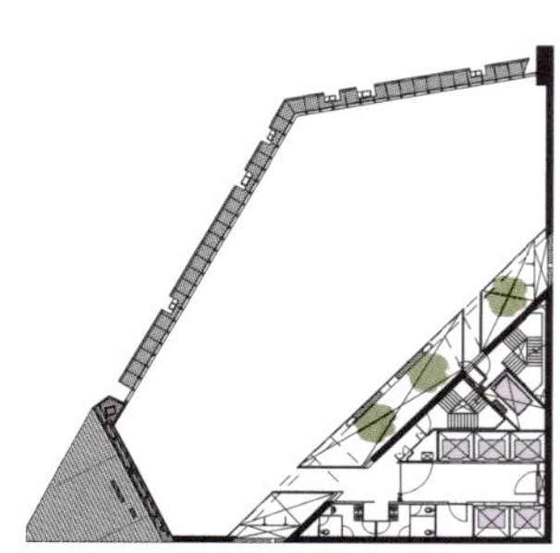

LEVEL 42

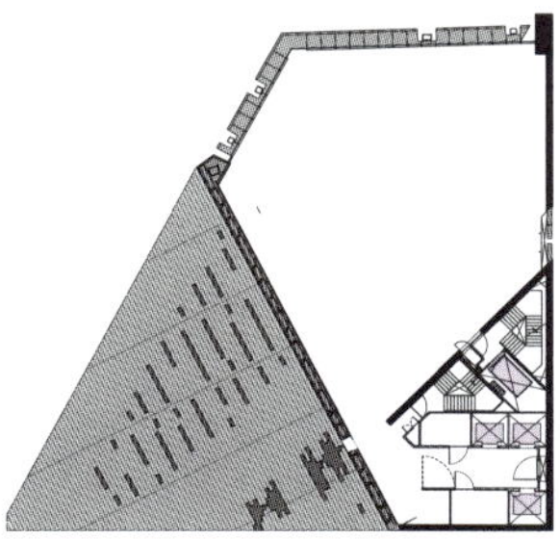

LEVEL 51

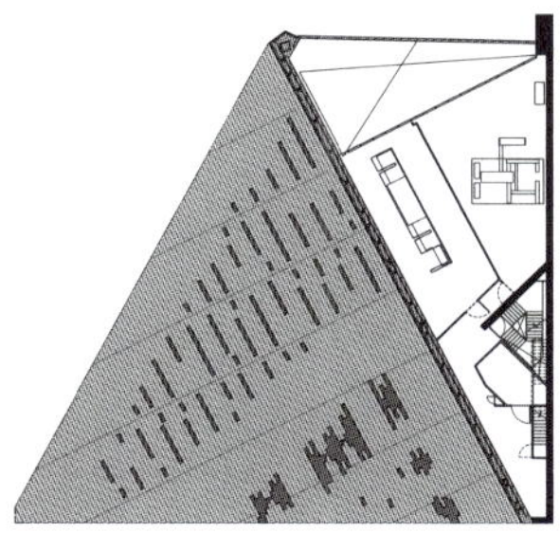

LEVEL 56

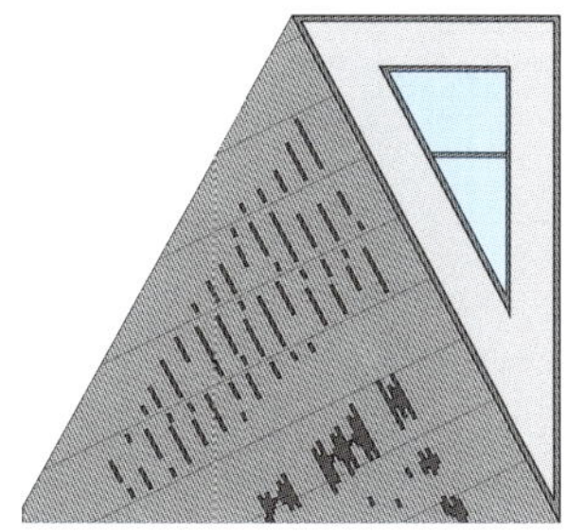

ROOFTOP

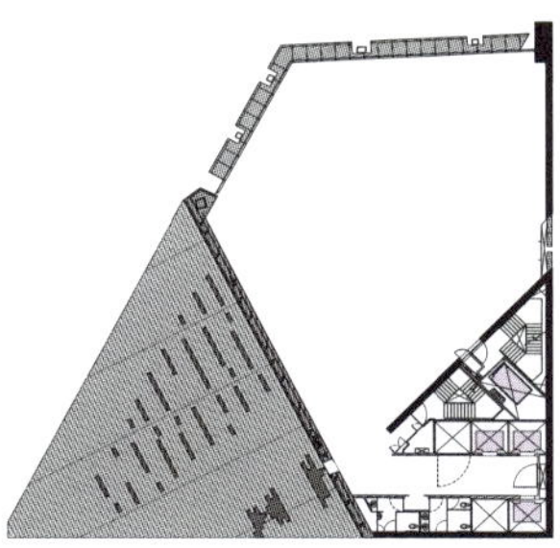

LEVEL 50

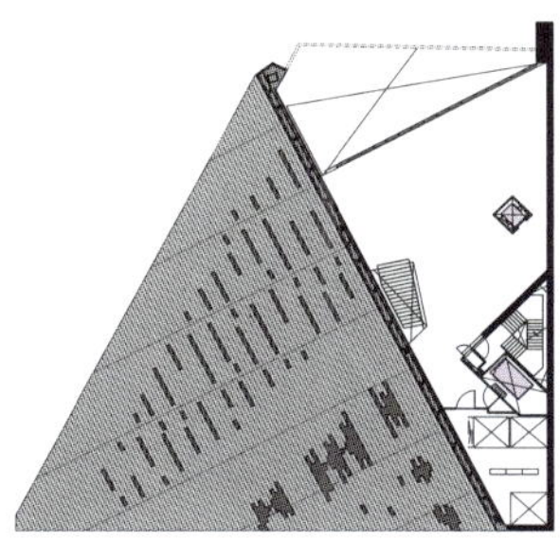

LEVEL 55

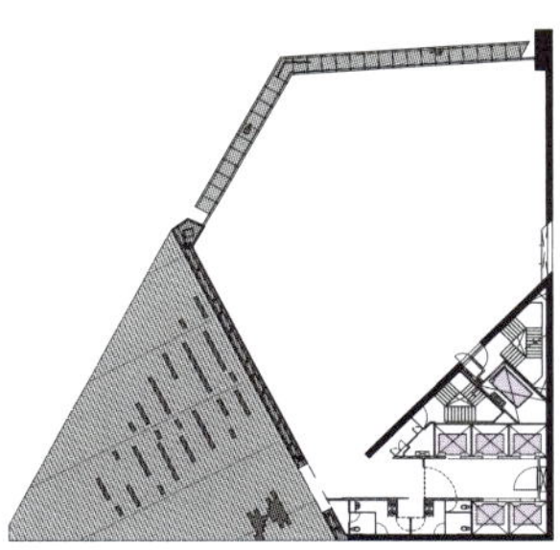

LEVEL 49

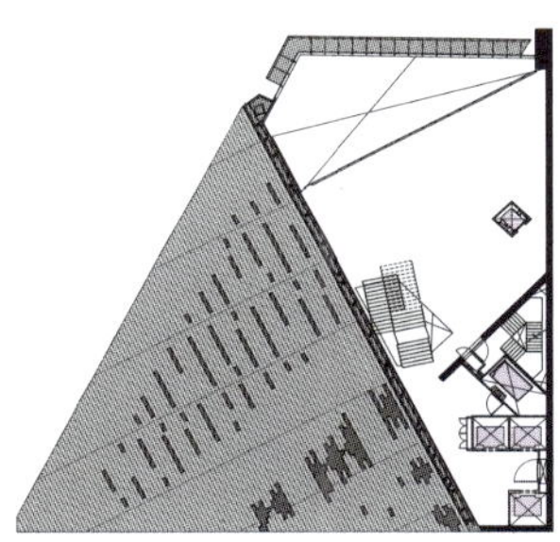

LEVEL 54

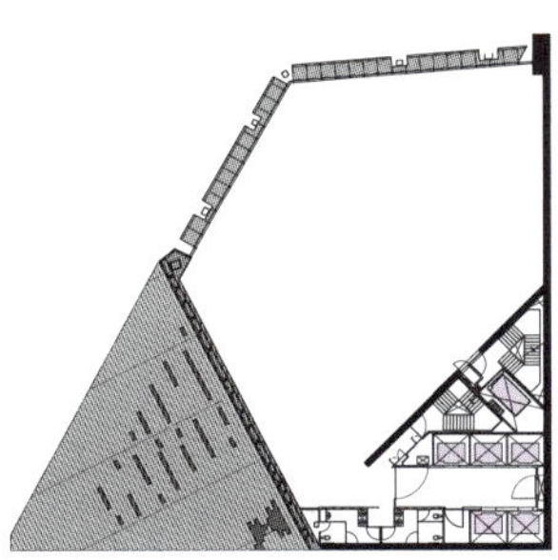

LEVEL 48

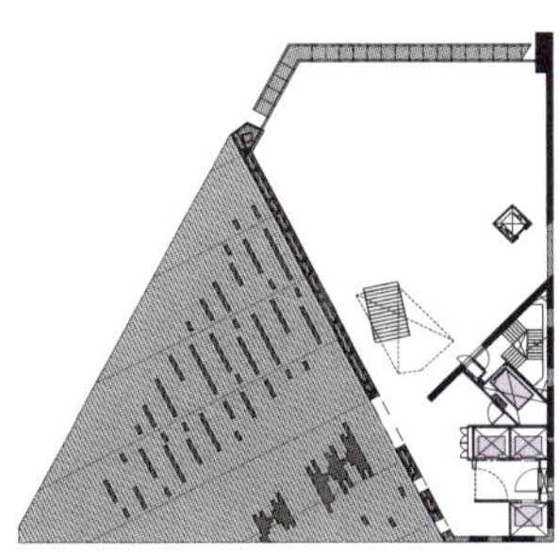

LEVEL 53

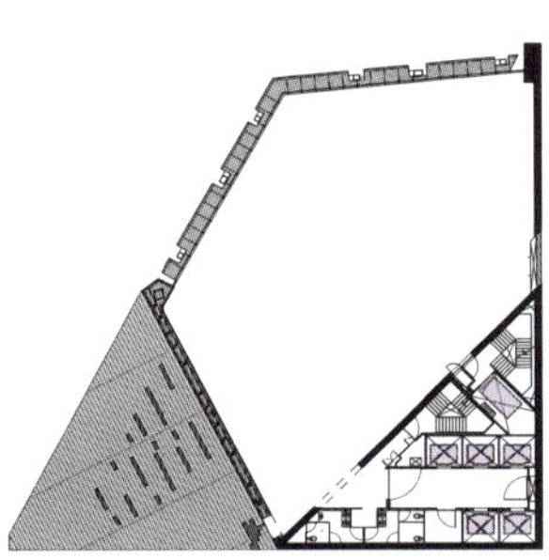

LEVEL 47

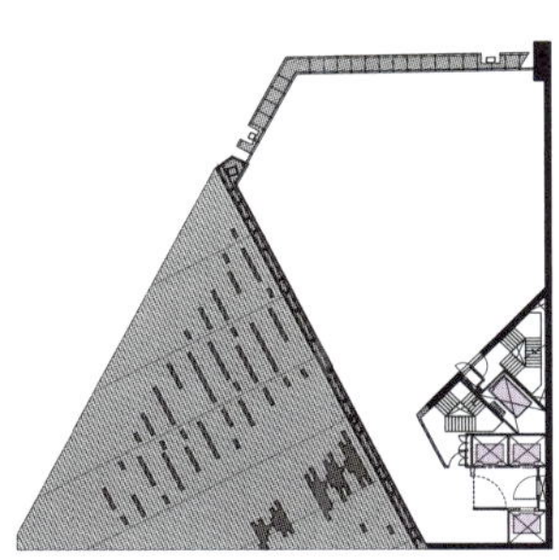

LEVEL 52

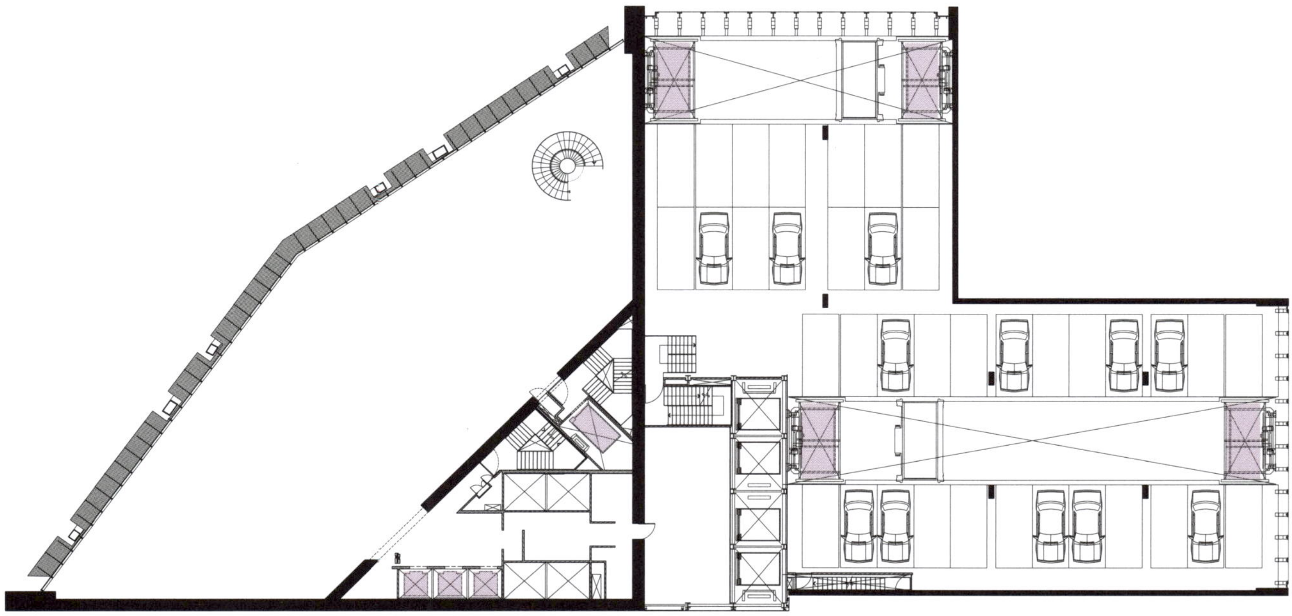

LEVEL 7

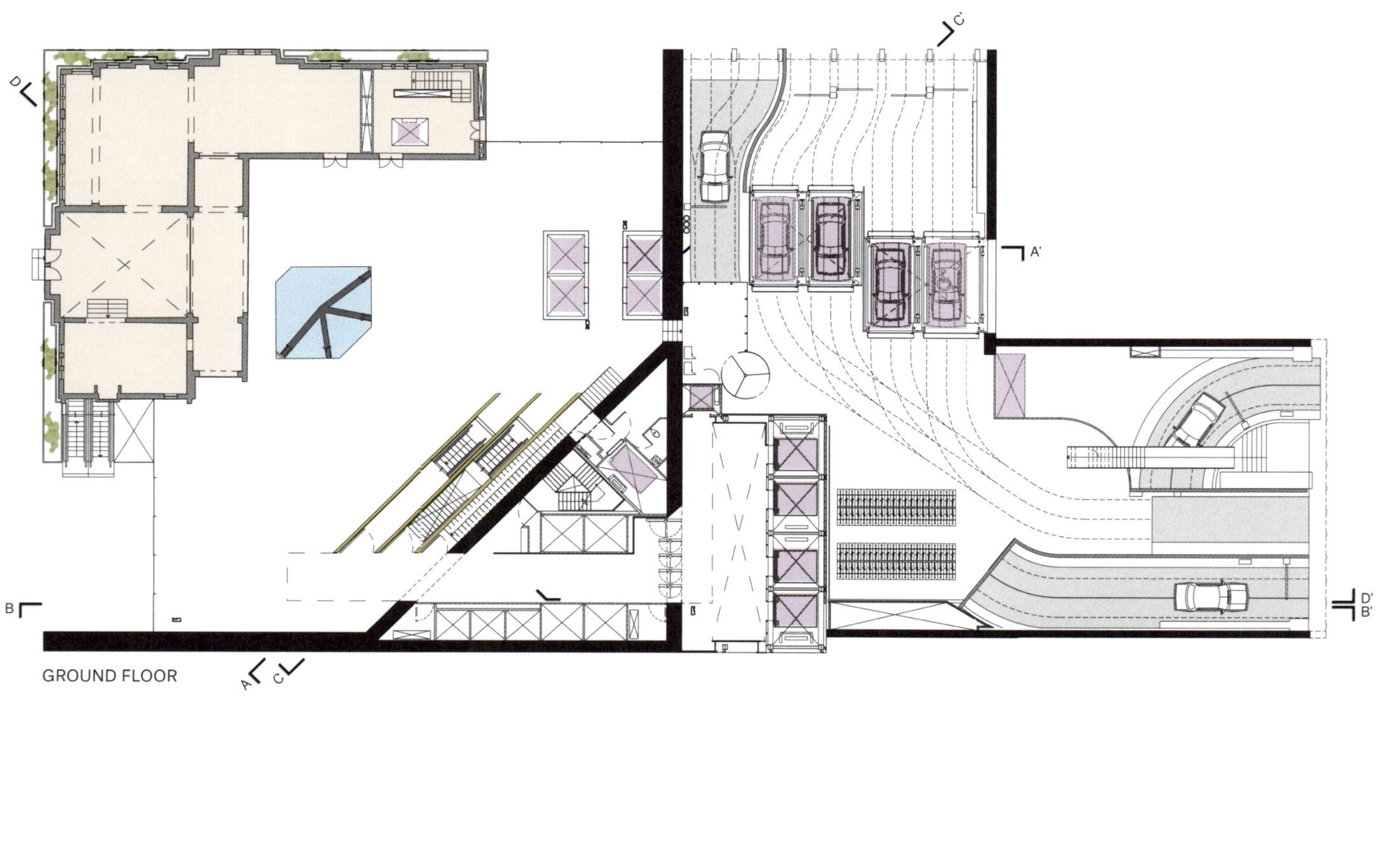

GROUND FLOOR

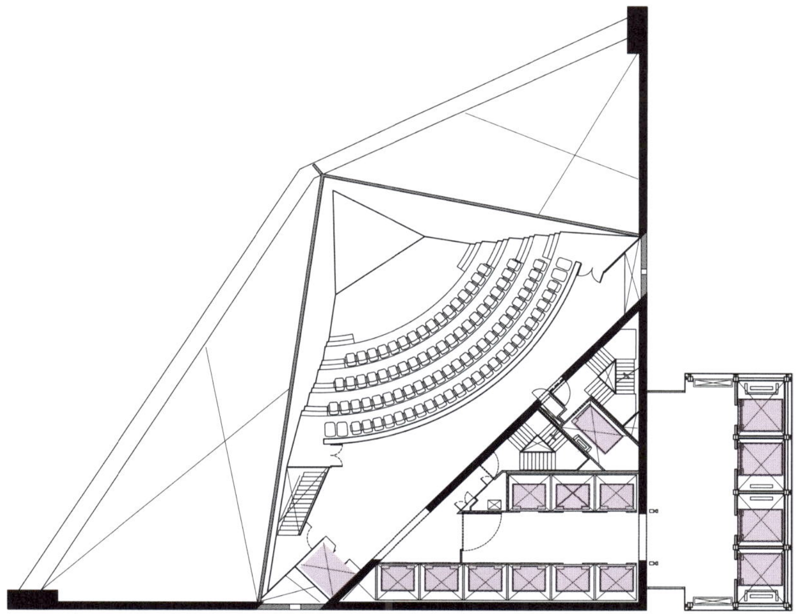

LEVEL 23 - Auditorium

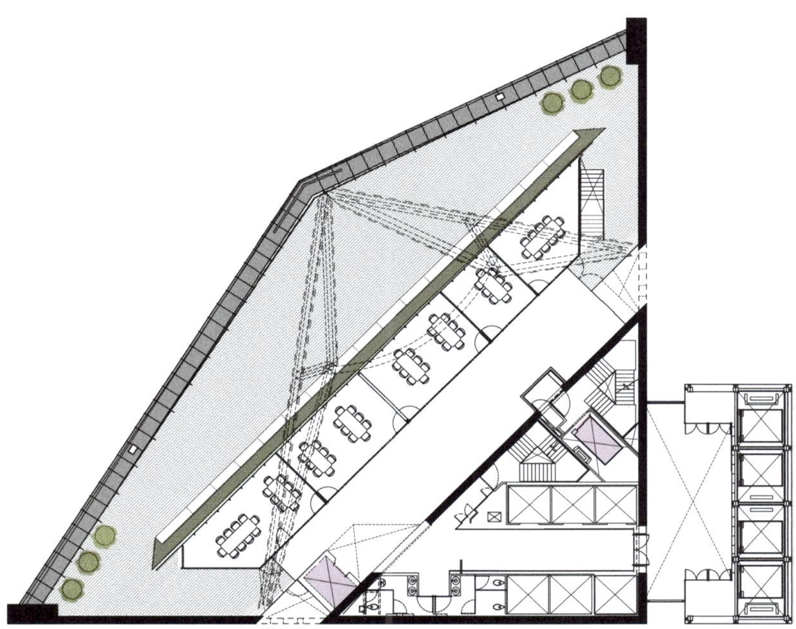

LEVEL 22 - Sky lobby

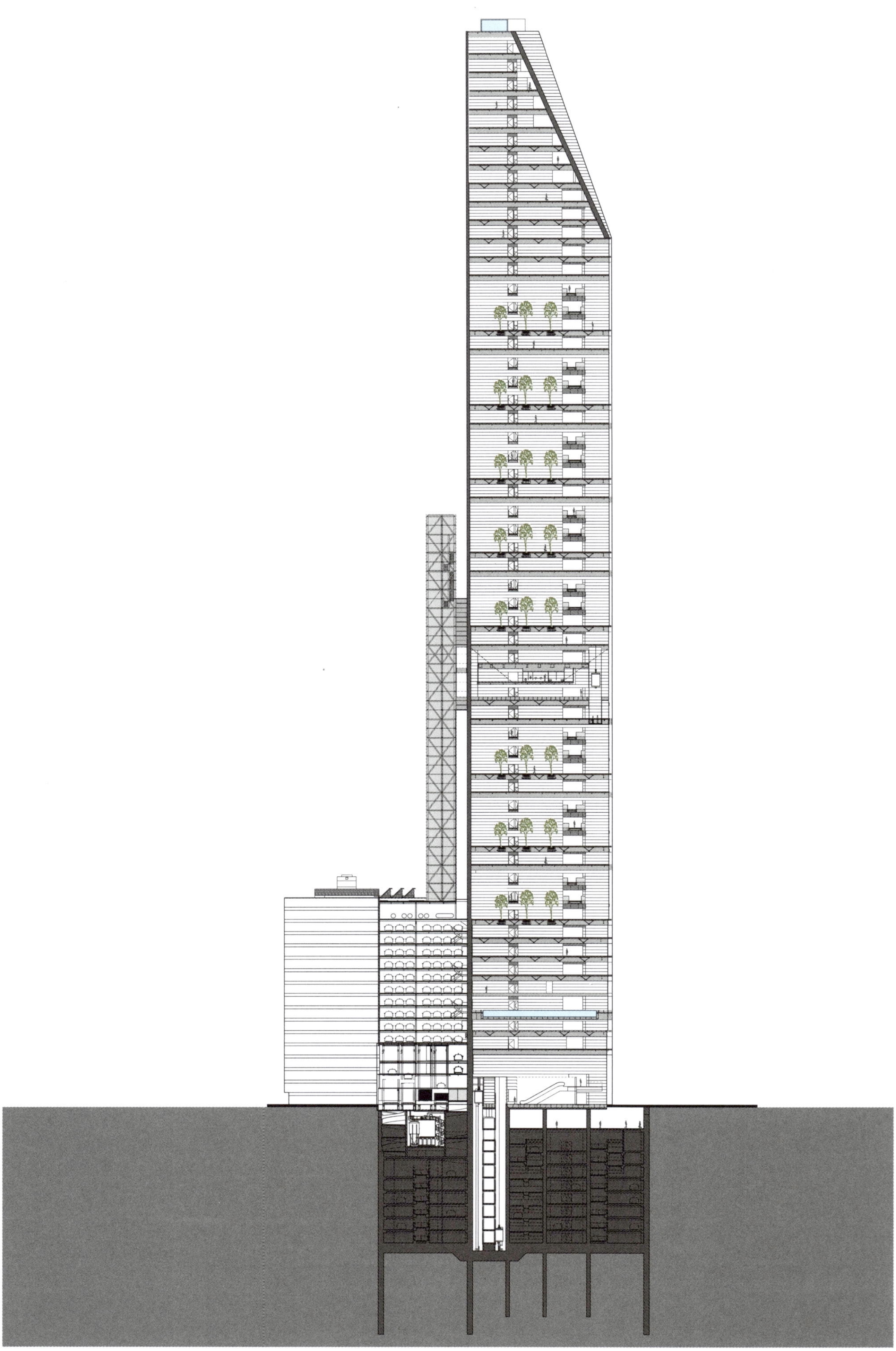

SECTION A–A'

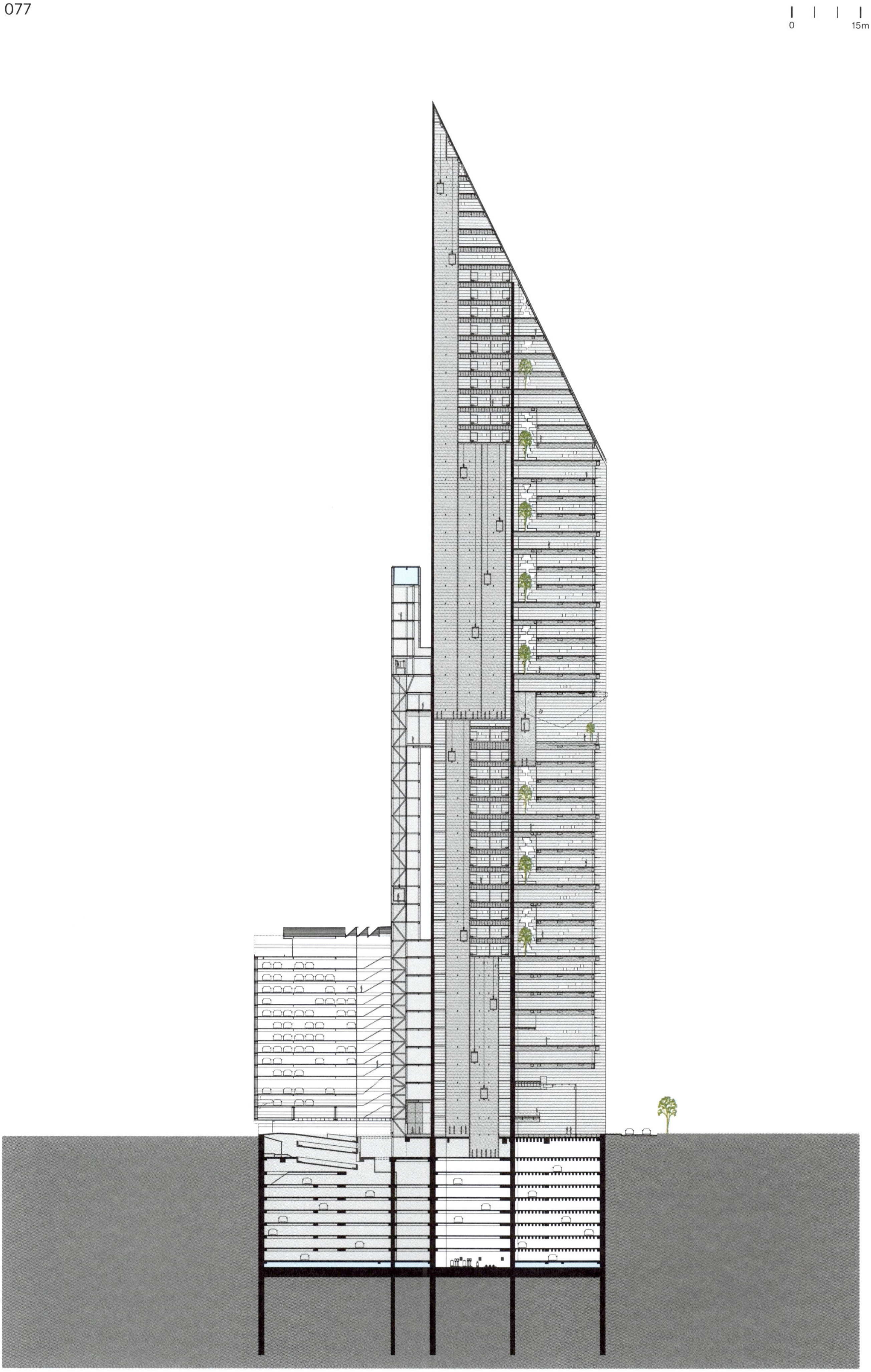

SECTION B-B'

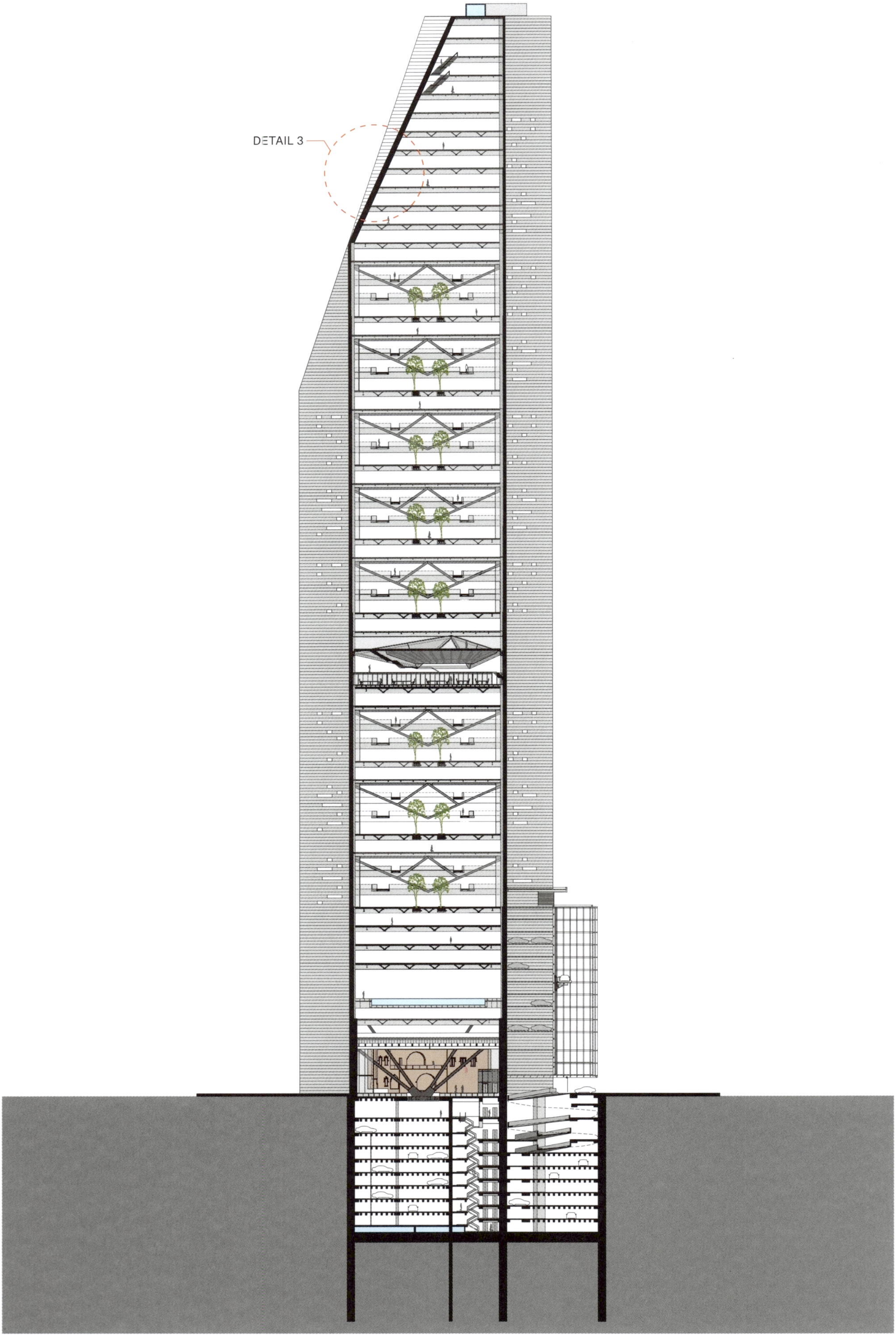

SECTION C–C'

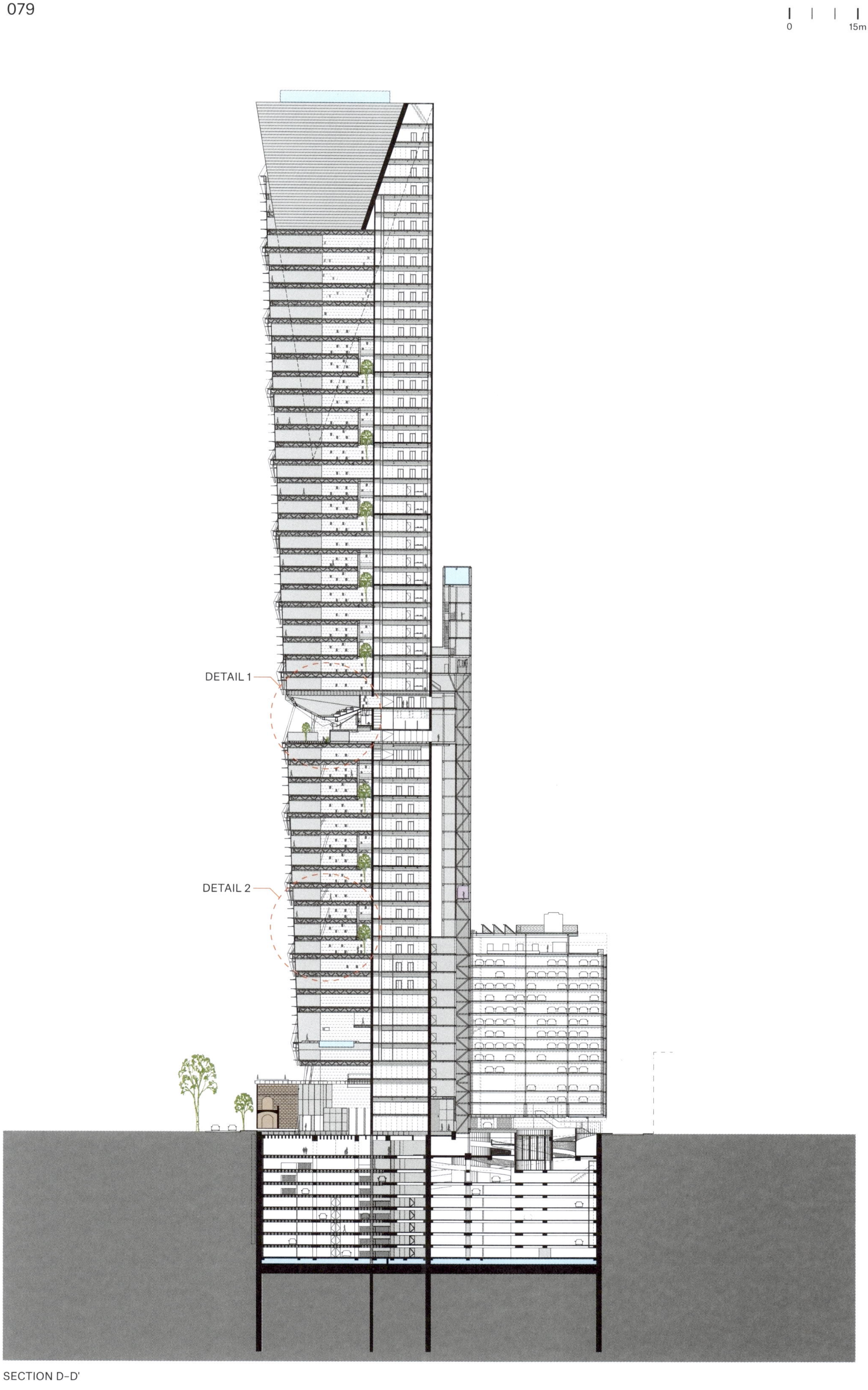

SECTION D-D'

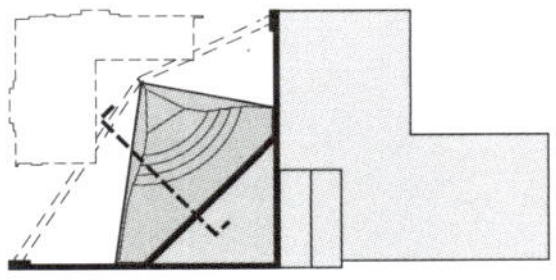

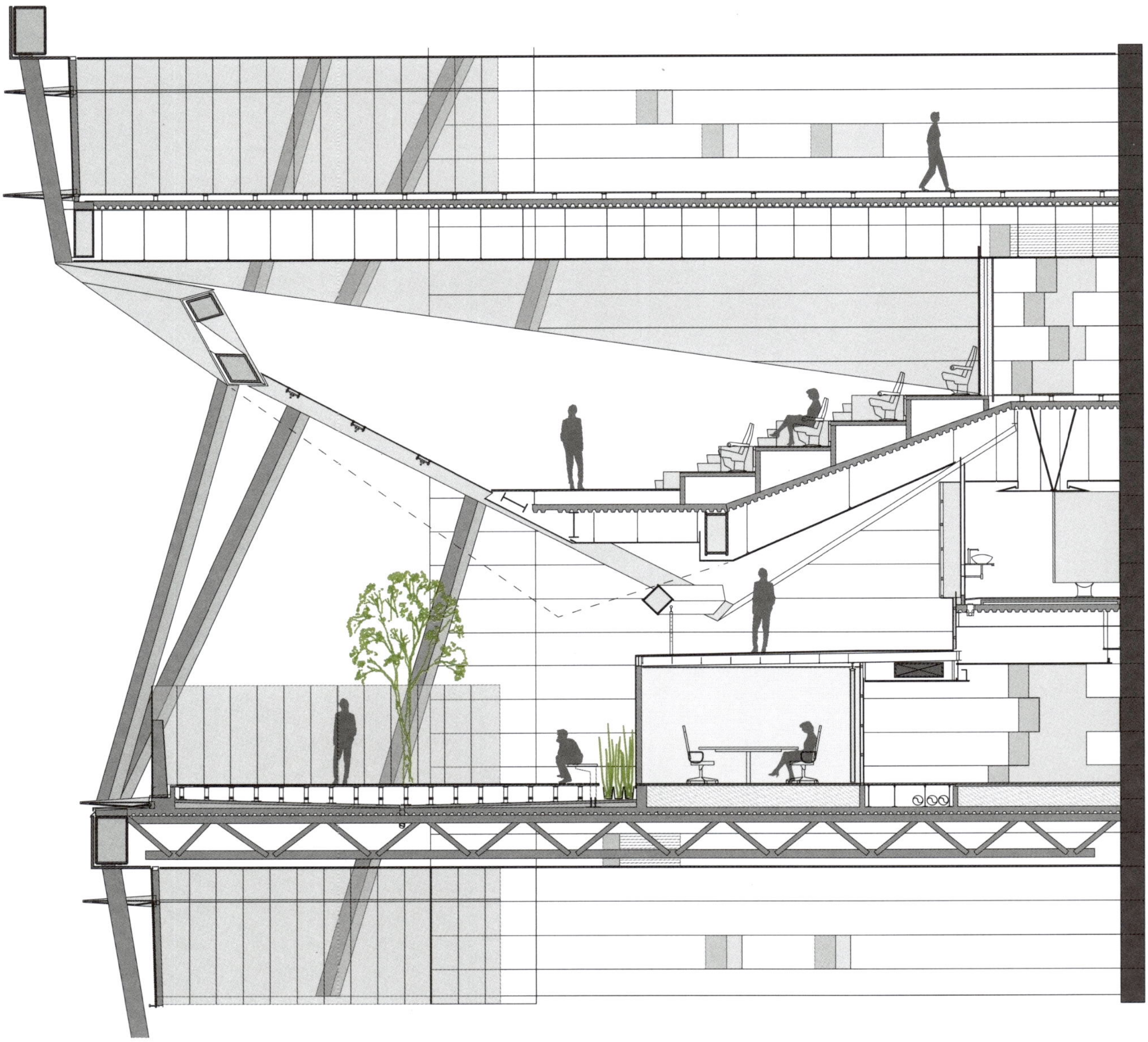

DETAIL 1
PARTIAL SECTION - Auditorium

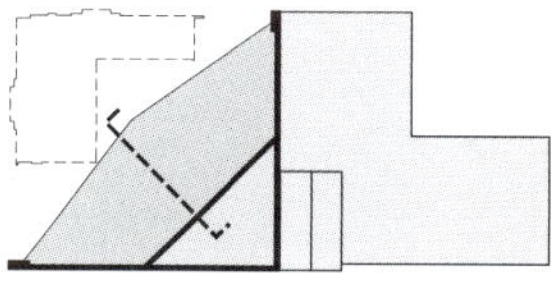

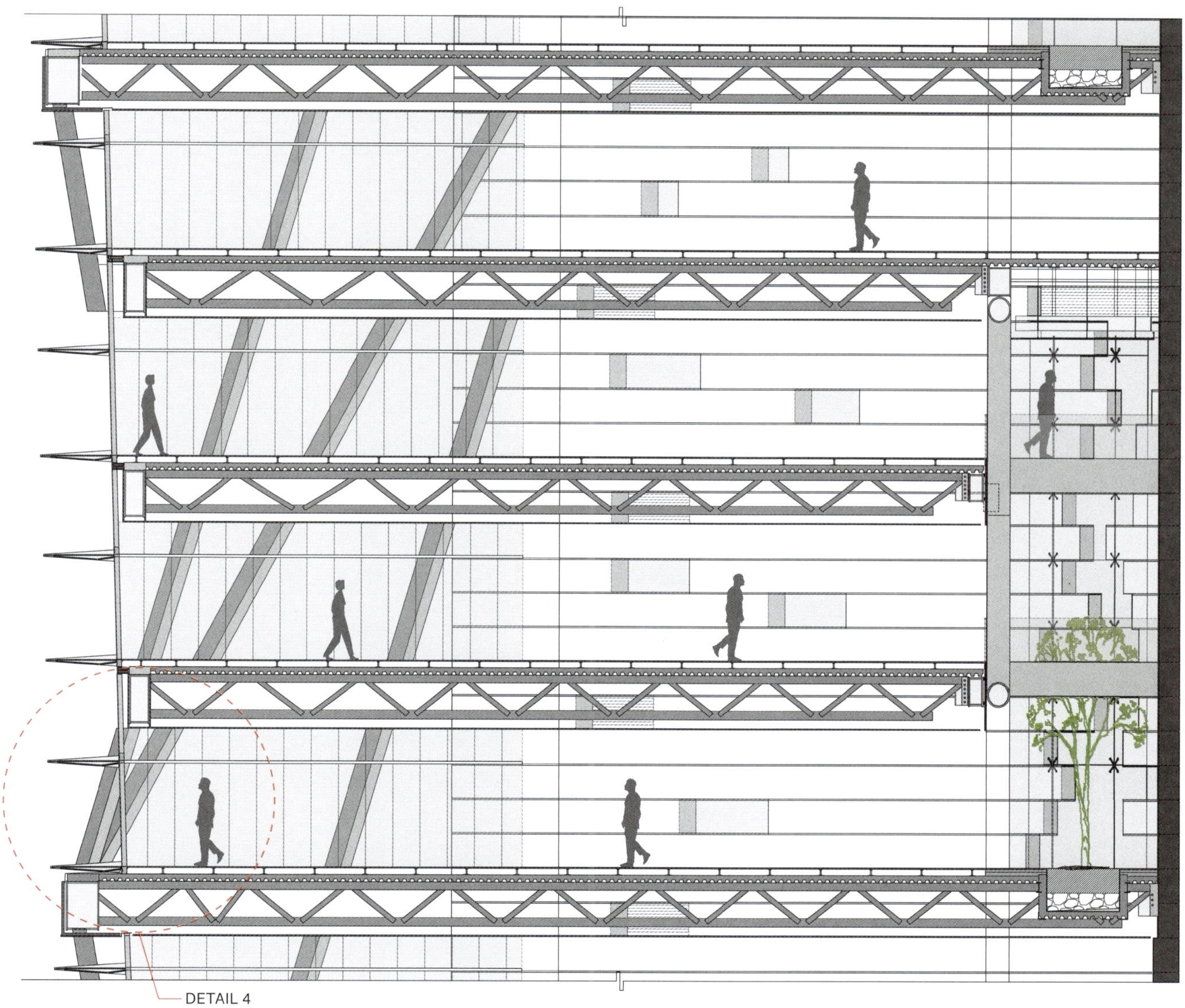

DETAIL 2
PARTIAL SECTION - Cluster 7

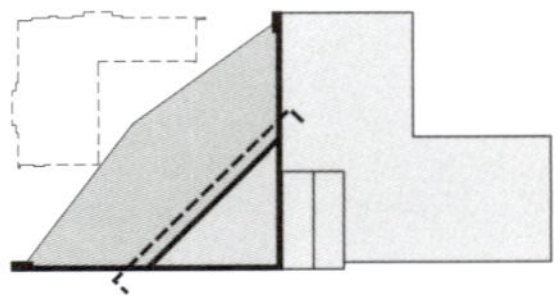

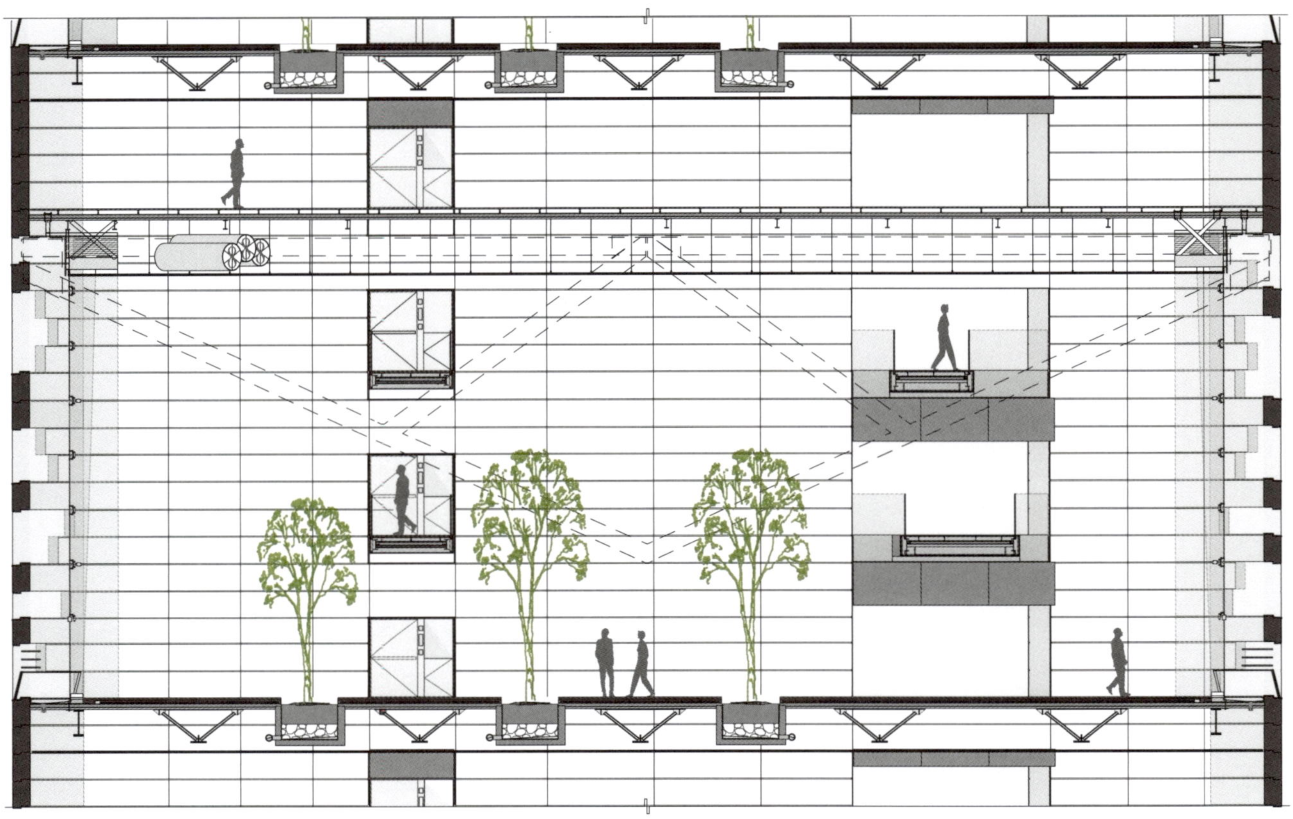

PARTIAL SECTION B - Cluster 7

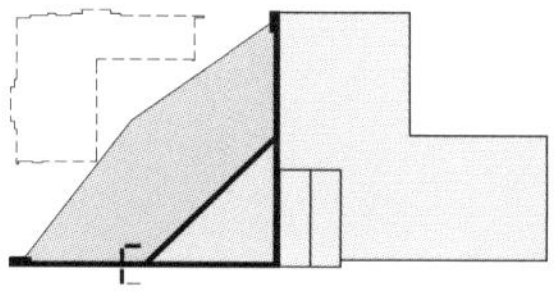

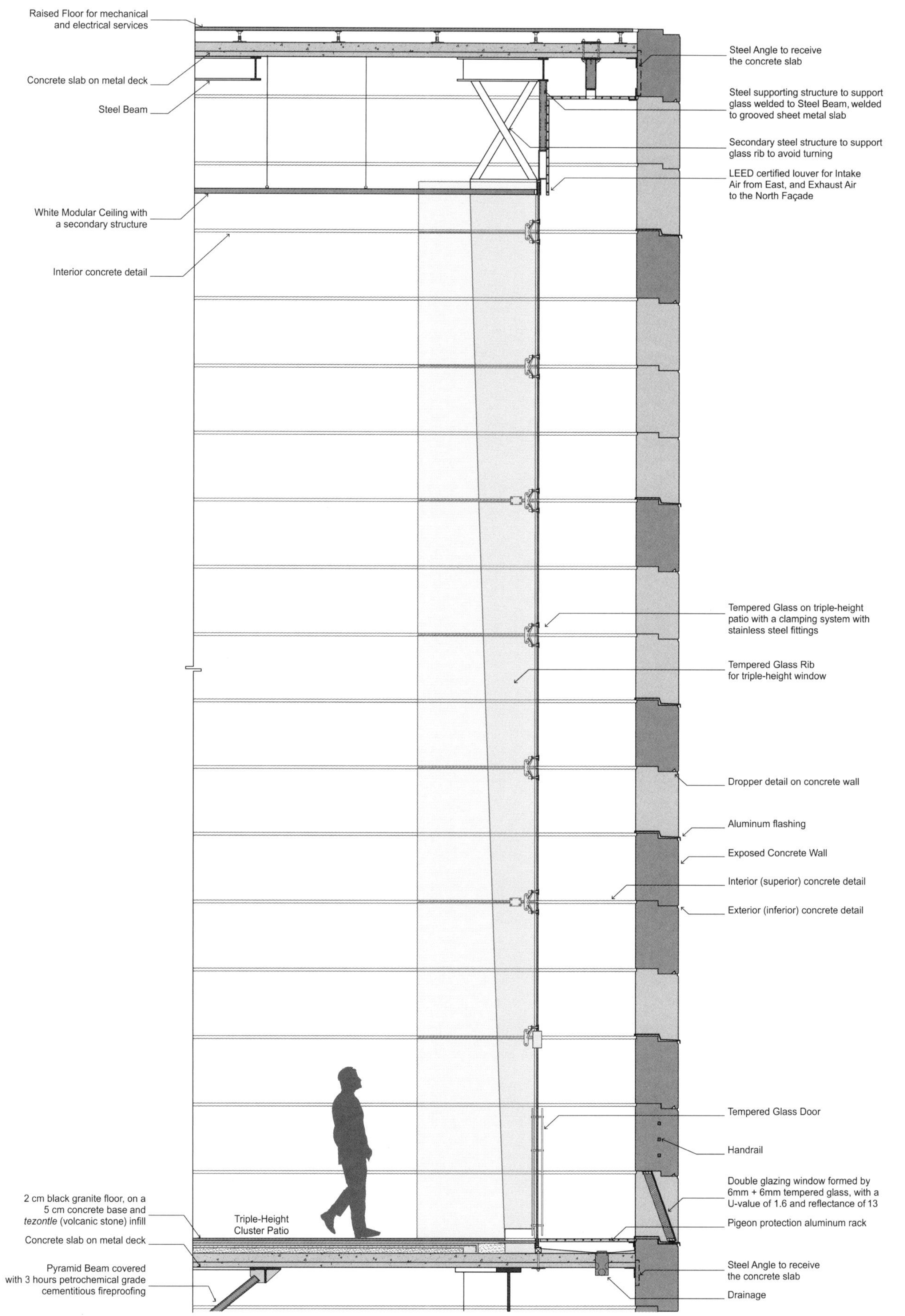

FAÇADE SECTION
CONCRETE WALL - Tetris

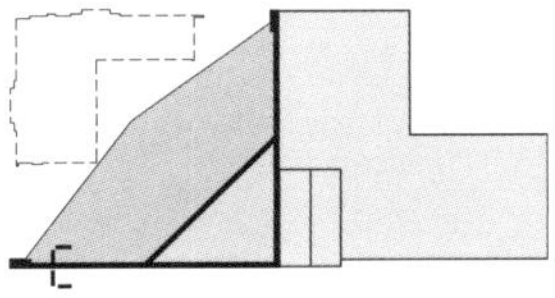

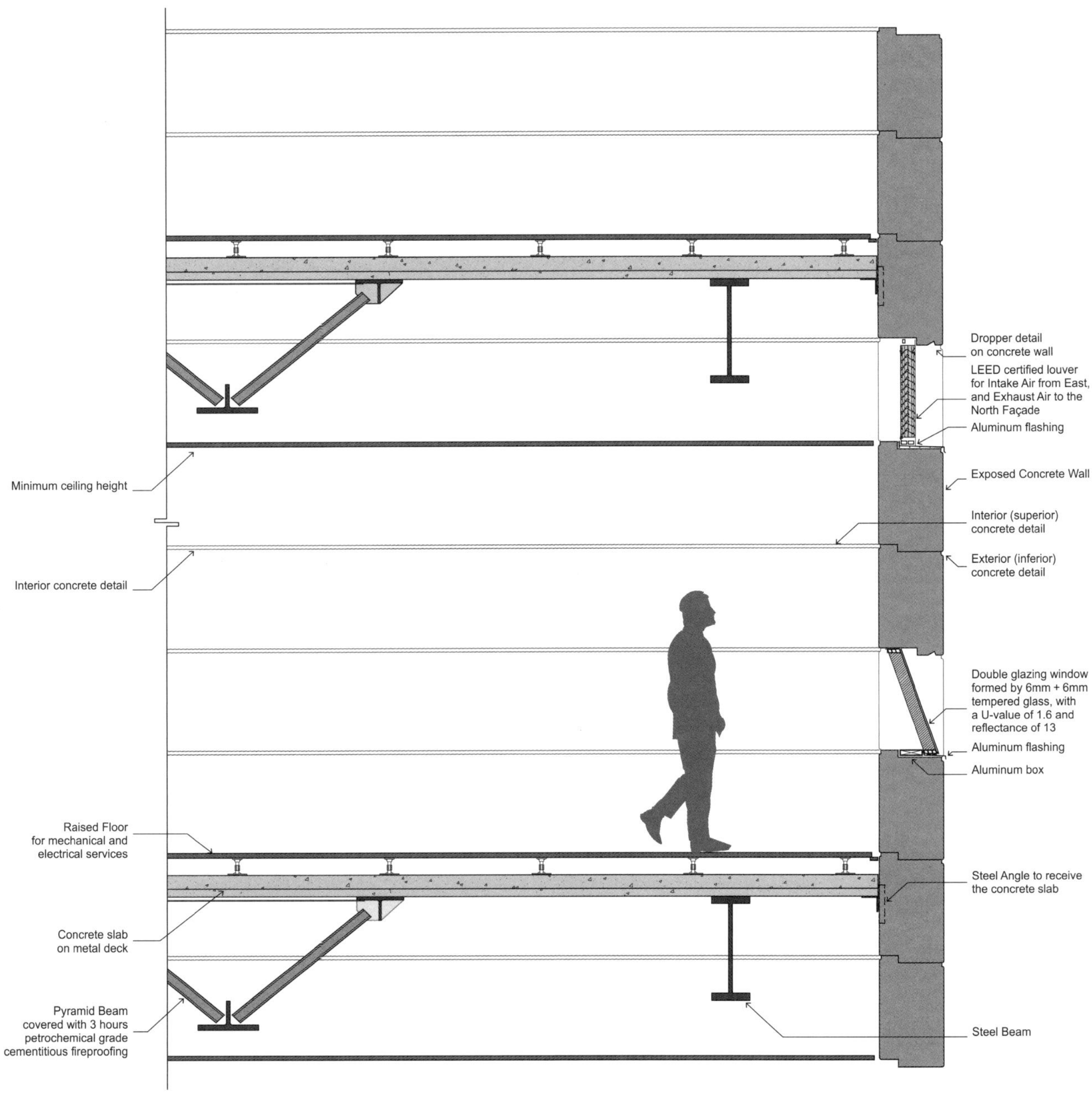

DETAILED SECTION
CONCRETE WALL - Window and Louver Detail

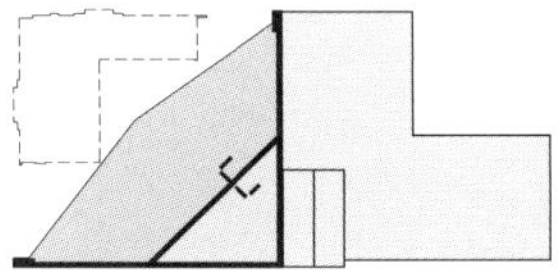

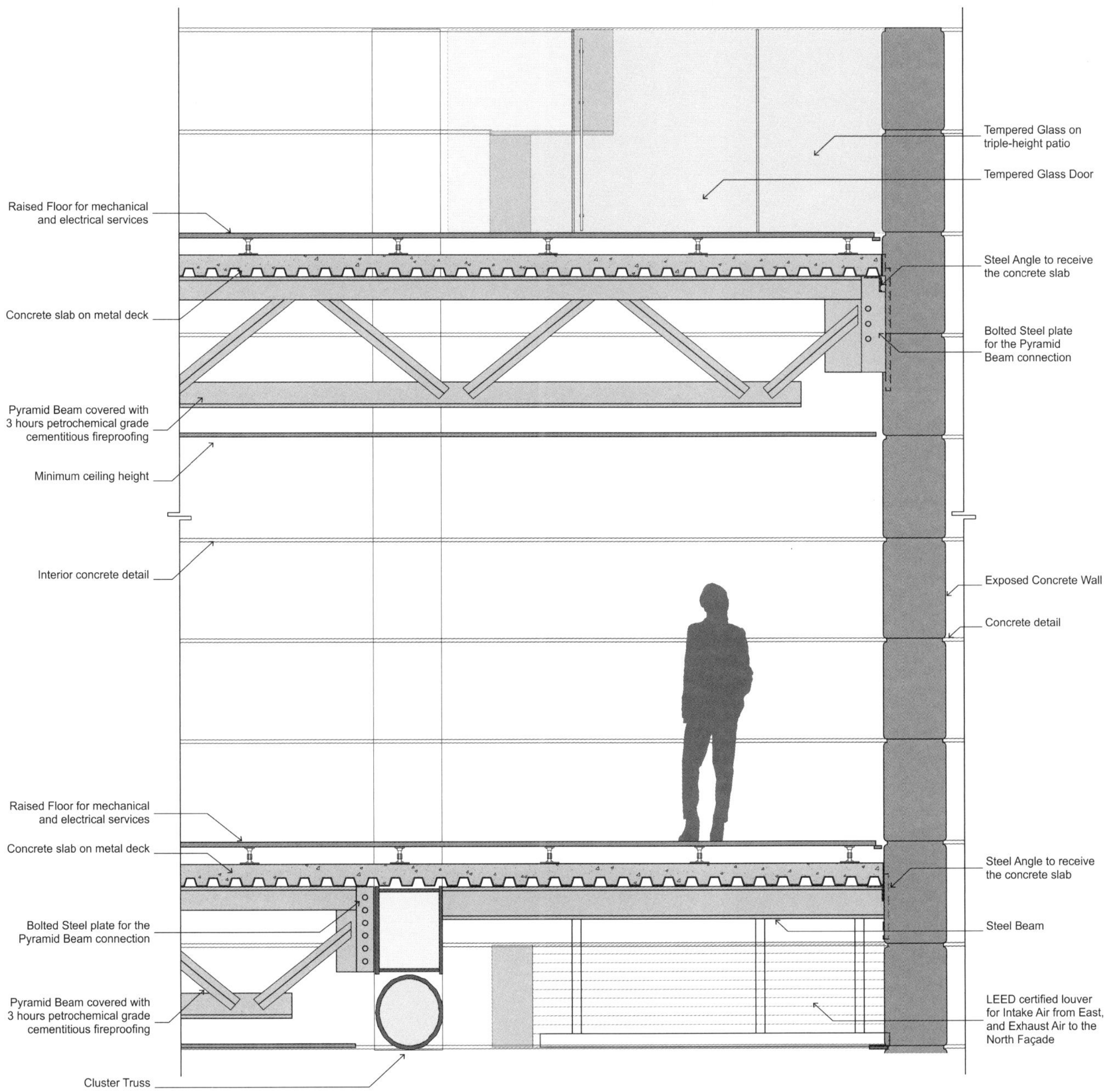

DETAILED SECTION
CONCRETE WALL

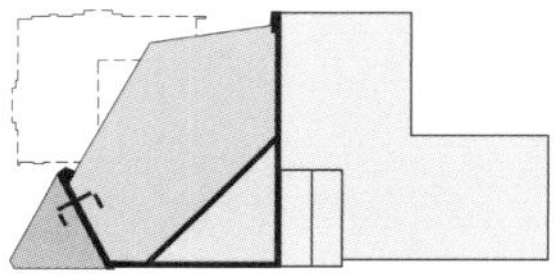

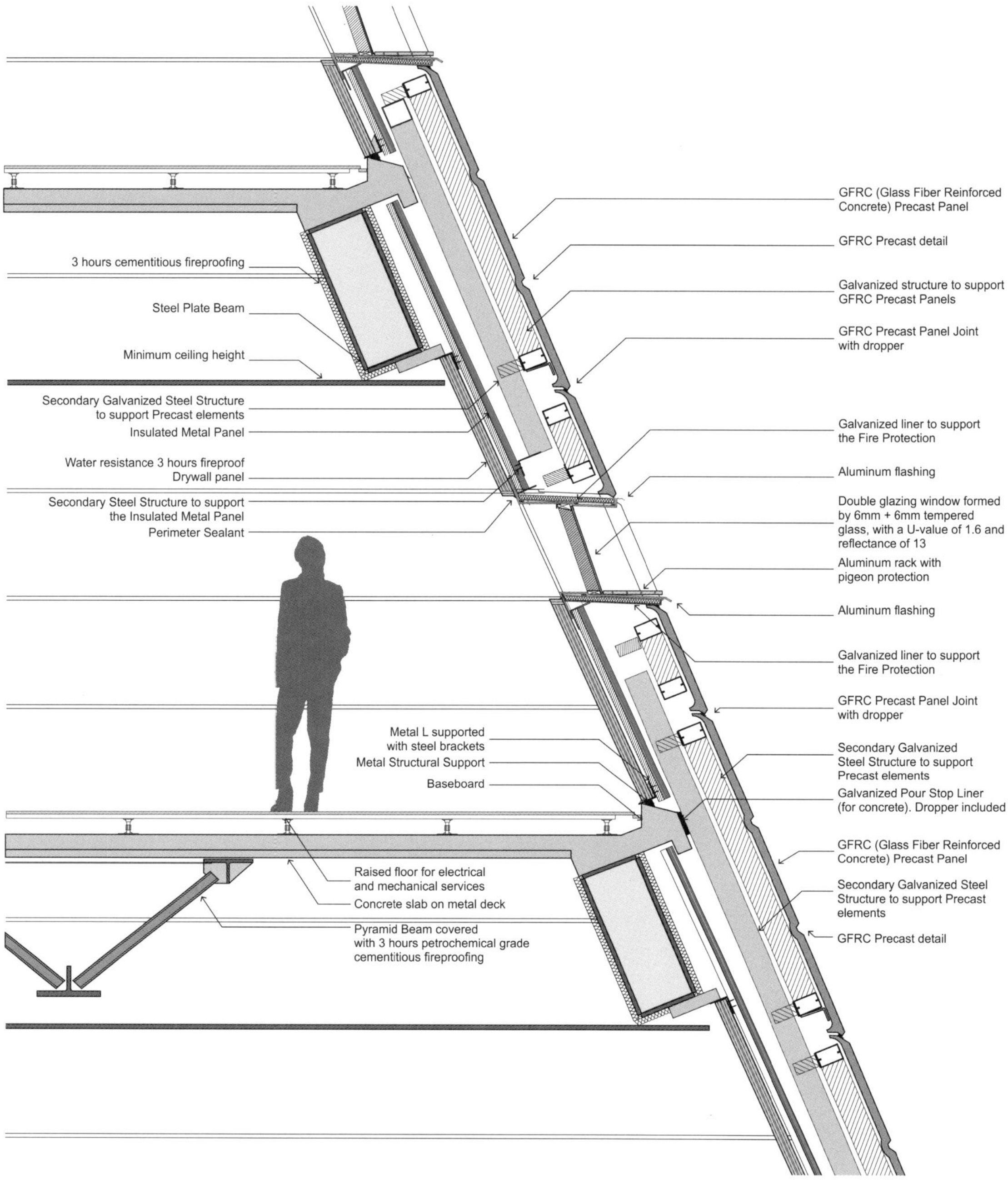

DETAIL 3
FAÇADE SECTION LEVEL 40 - Precast window elements

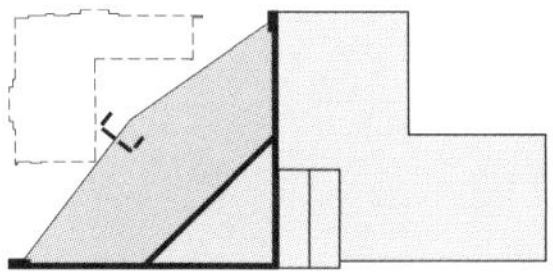

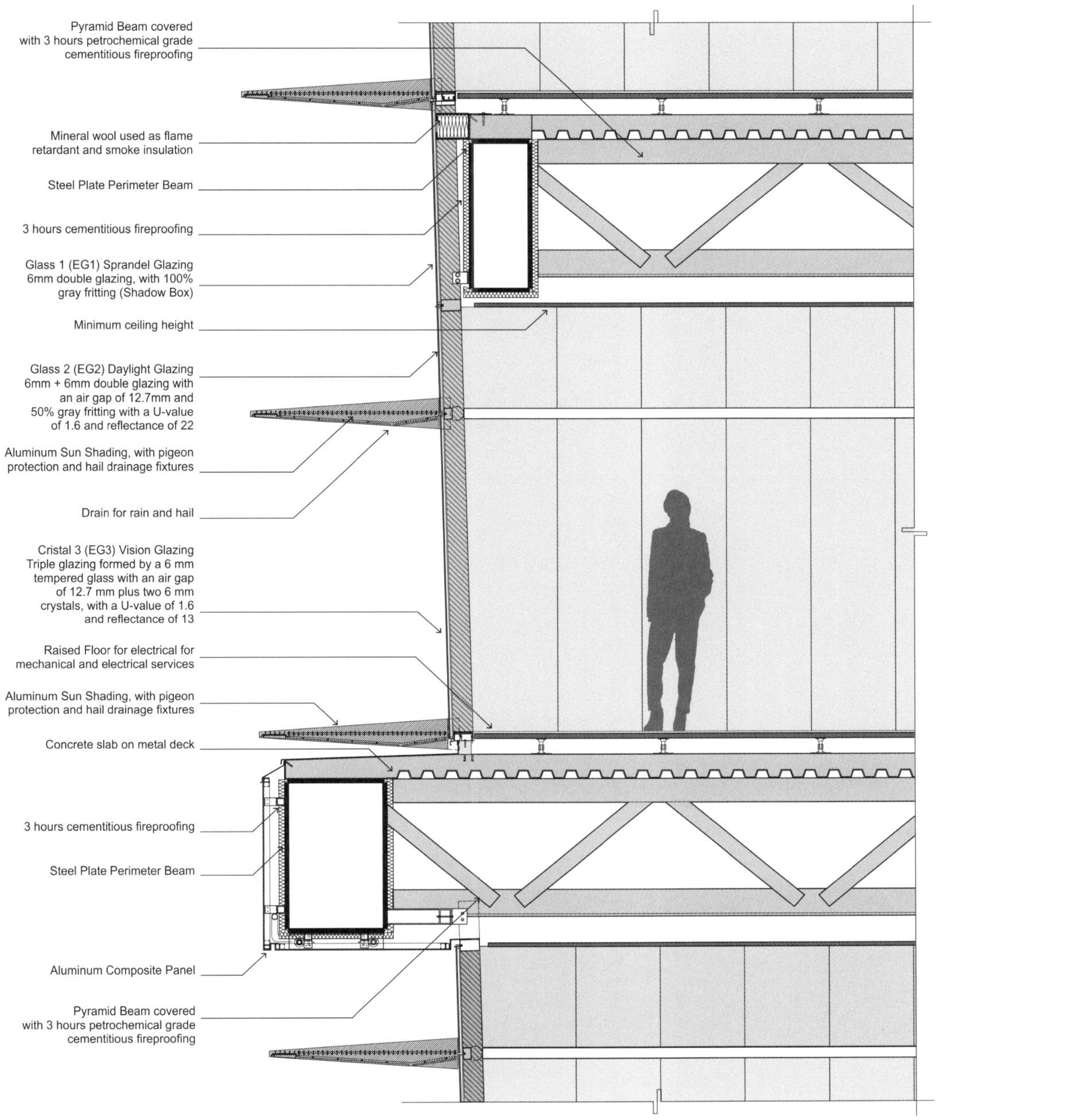

DETAIL 4
FAÇADE SECTION LEVEL 25 - Glass façade

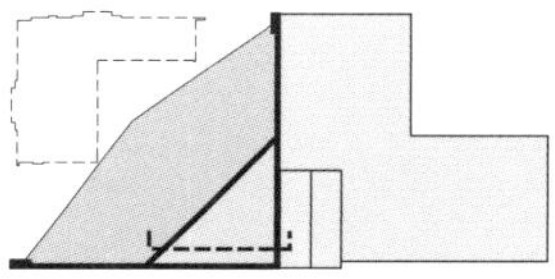

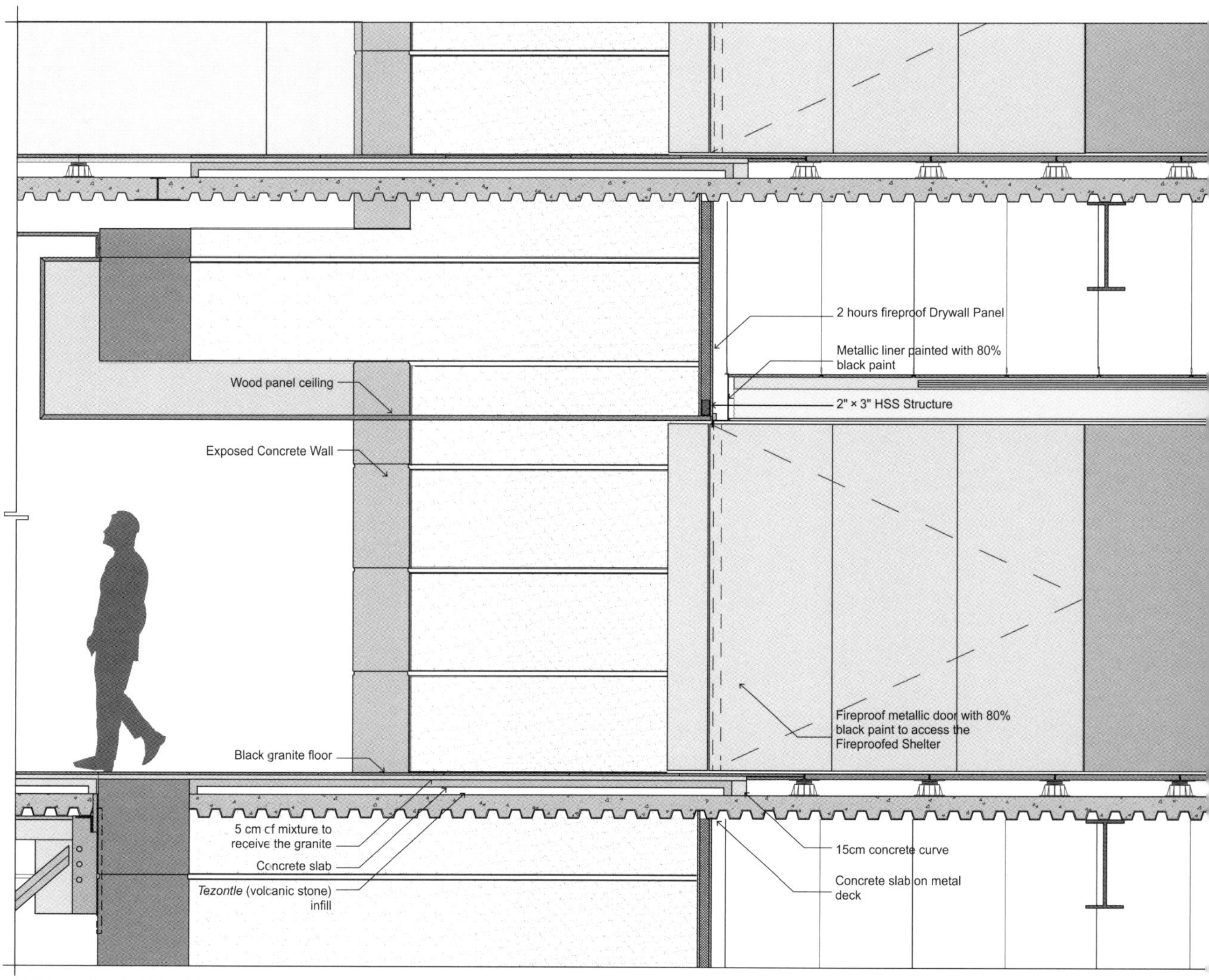

LONGITUDINAL SECTION
ELEVATOR LOBBY

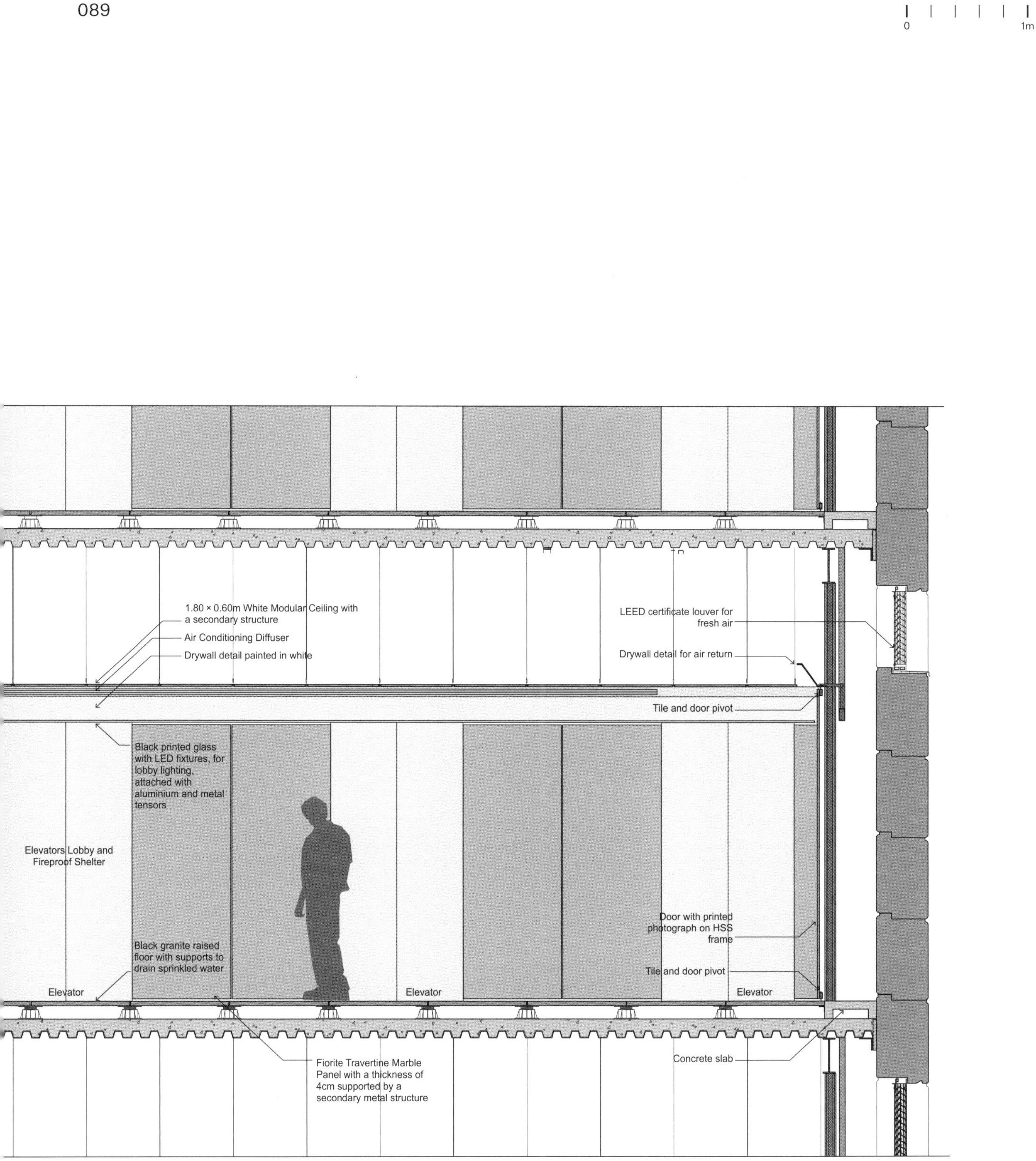
0
1m
1.80 × 0.60m White Modular Ceiling with a secondary structure
Air Conditioning Diffuser
Drywall detail painted in white
LEED certificate louver for fresh air
Drywall detail for air return
Tile and door pivot
Black printed glass with LED fixtures, for lobby lighting, attached with aluminium and metal tensors
Elevators Lobby and Fireproof Shelter
Door with printed photograph on HSS frame
Black granite raised floor with supports to drain sprinkled water
Tile and door pivot
Elevator
Elevator
Elevator
Concrete slab
Fiorite Travertine Marble Panel with a thickness of 4cm supported by a secondary metal structure

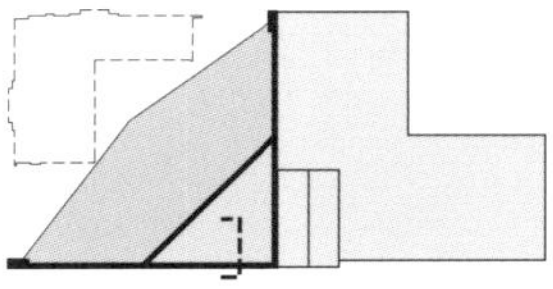

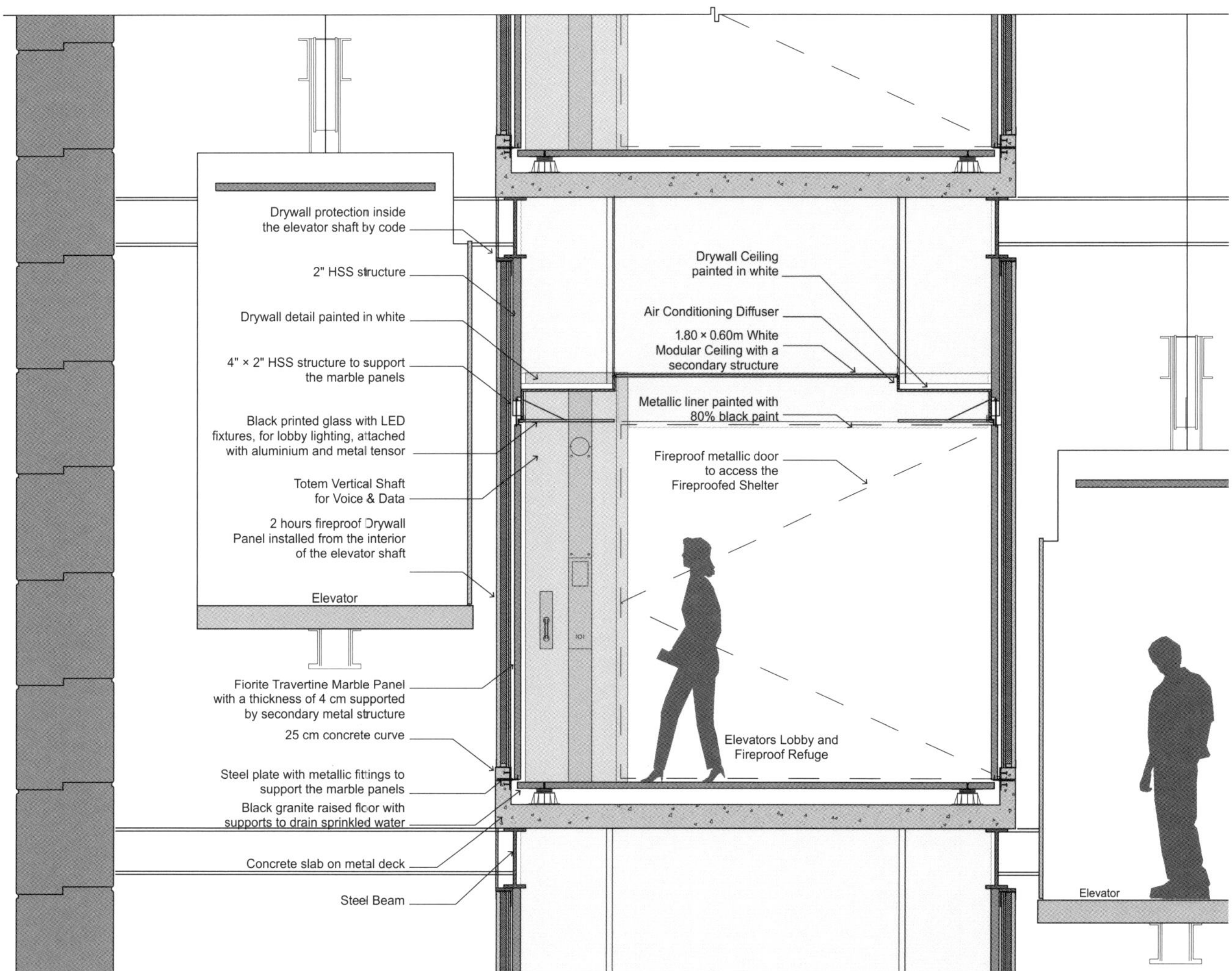

TRANSVERSAL SECTION
ELEVATOR LOBBY

0 0.5m

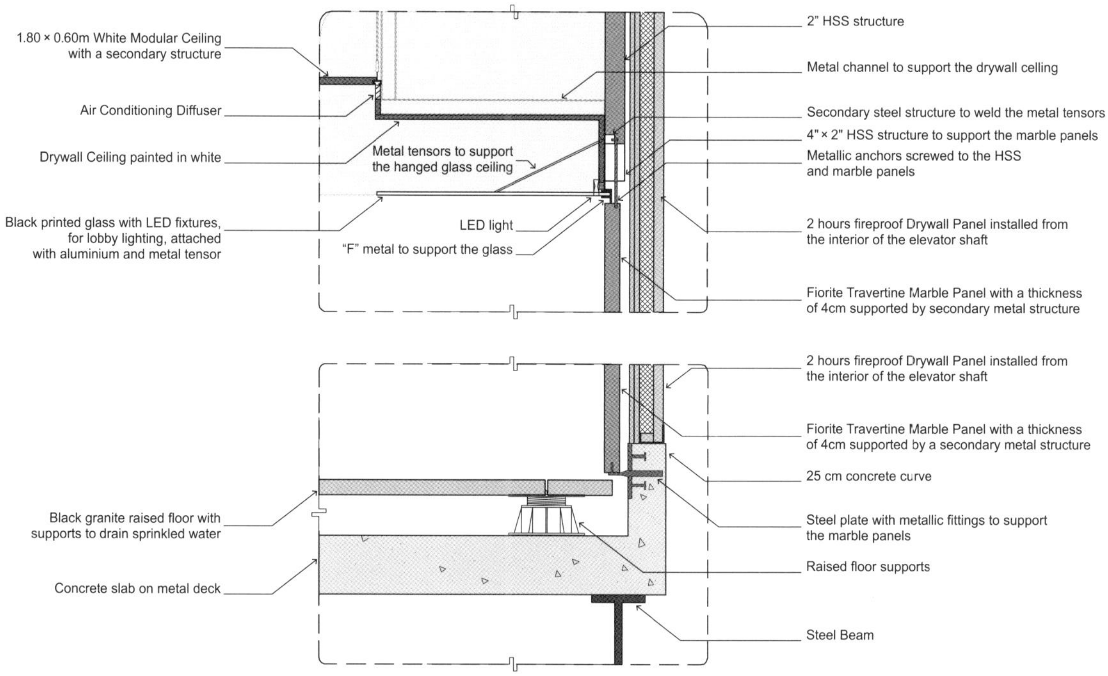

DETAIL LAMP - Marble
ELEVATOR LOBBY

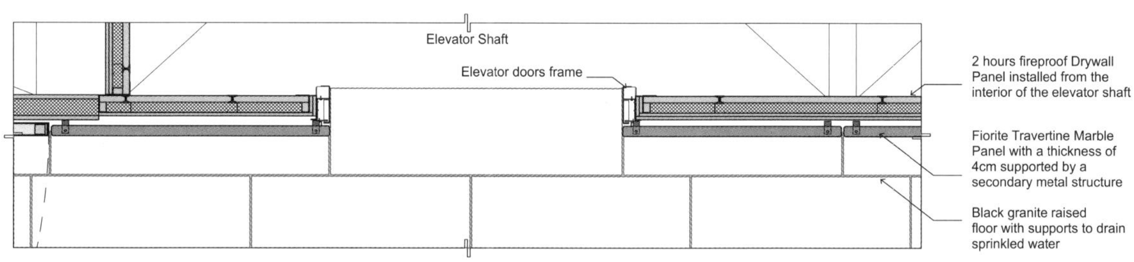

DETAIL ELEVATOR DOOR
ELEVATOR LOBBY

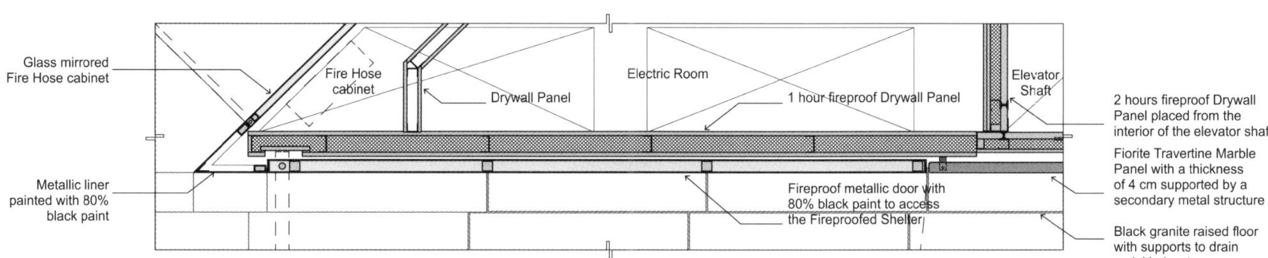

DETAIL EMERGENCY DOOR
ELEVATOR LOBBY

The glass sloped façade accumulates an inclination of 14 meters through the total height of the building, which compromising the design, the construction process and the building façade cleaning system Gondola.

When we embarked on the façade design of the warped surface, we received many different ideas, including a proposal by Gehry Technologies Company that pretended to rationalize the façade modules through algorithms. Their goal was to identify the minimal identical module family groups, with a minimal set of mullions and glass types, to obtain the desired curvature of the façade.

The best proposal we received, suggested a maximum of ten different module families, but the number was too big for the façade manufacturer, as well as for the final user building administrator, due to the impossibility of producing or storing enough panes of glass with the original technical specifications, which involved specific tinting of the glass, to allow for breakage or damage over the lifetime of the building. Standardizing the façade modules saves time and money and facilitates a long-lasting building image.

I have designed and developed along with Fernando Hernández many different façades, for which we have achieved specific solutions for unique situations. The warped façade of Torre Reforma was not an exception. We accomplished the design of a single module for the entire the building with a single assembly type to obtain the desired curvature of the façade.

The vertical mullions overlap differently in each window, adjusting the module inclination by allowing the individuality of each module in each floor to the required slope. The designed mullion was used for the entire façade including the intermediate façade module, where the different slopes are adjusted. The solution was given by customizing the glass sizes with the same mullion at the point where the different inclined facades meet.

The first mullion-glass panel is installed vertically as the concrete wall is, allowing the following mullion-glass panel to incline as required, by adjusting in each module the required slope, giving form to the designed warping façade.

The accumulative difference in the vertical measurement of the difference on the inclination is absorbed at the top of each cluster, where the façade meets the structural exposed beam, at the same point where the cleaning gondola rail is located. This rail runs horizontal in each cluster, minimizing the cantilevered difference created by gravity and the building overhang.

In my opinion, the construction challenge of a curve and sloped tall building façade may find a better solution by splitting up the problem, rather than accumulating exaggerated deformations of the construction.

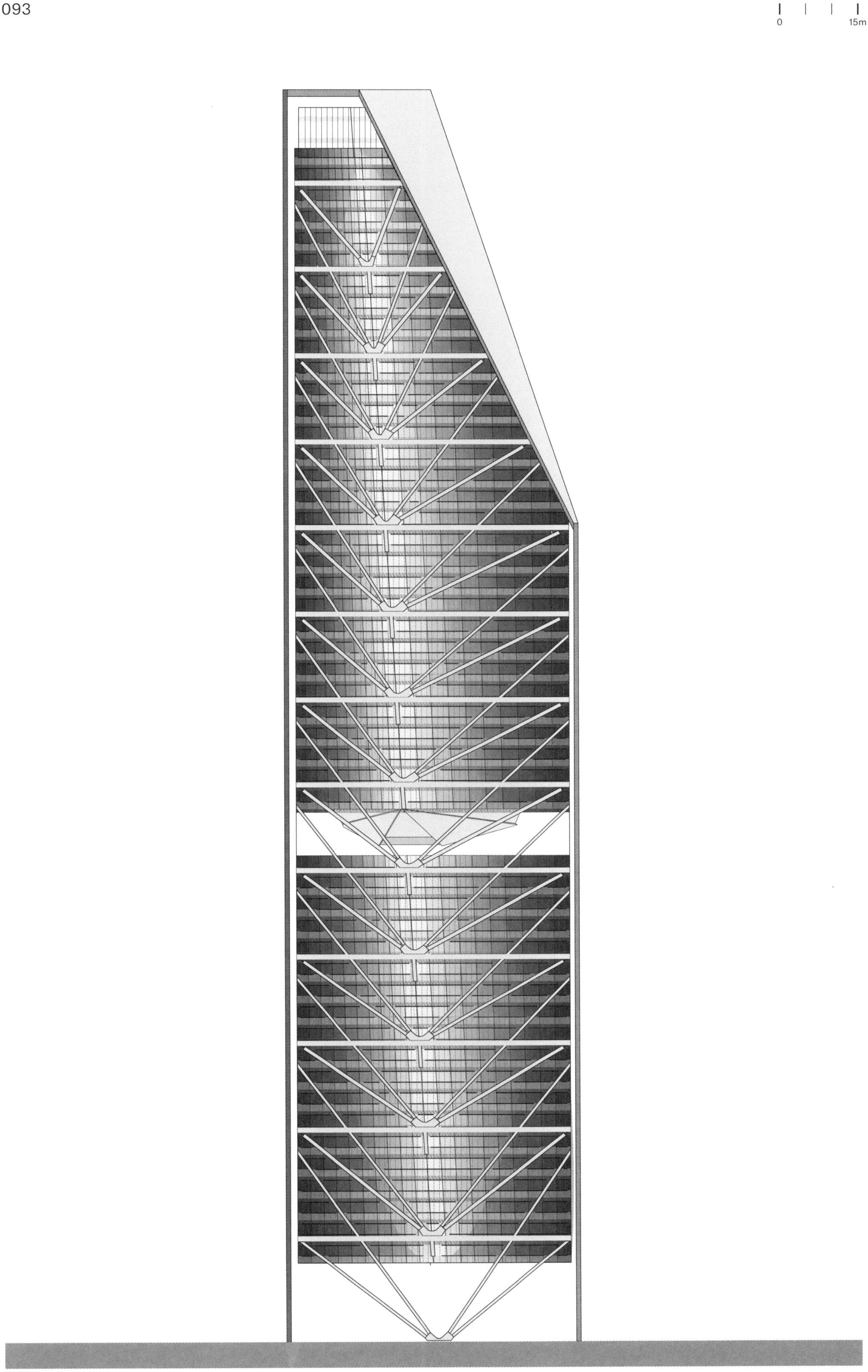

GLASS FAÇADE

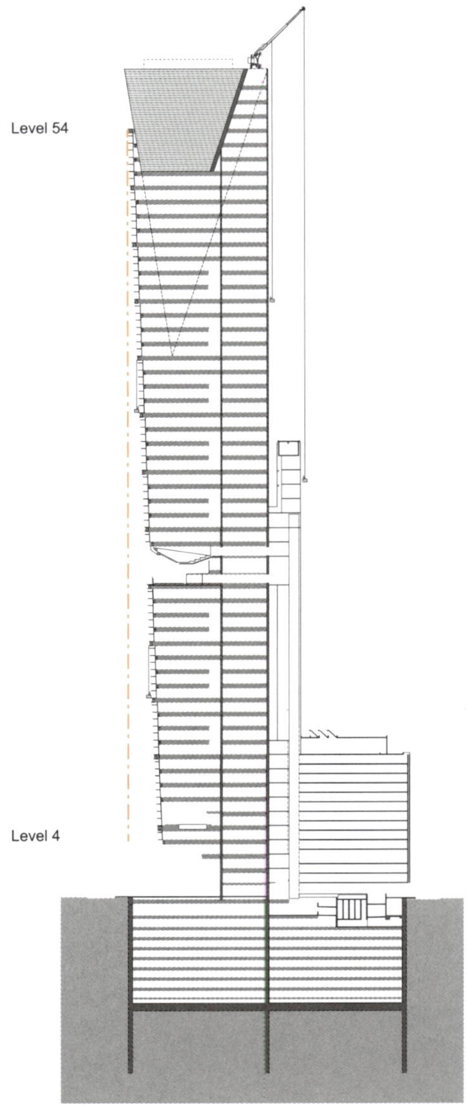

SCHEMATIC SECTION
14.00 m OVERHANG AND GONDOLA

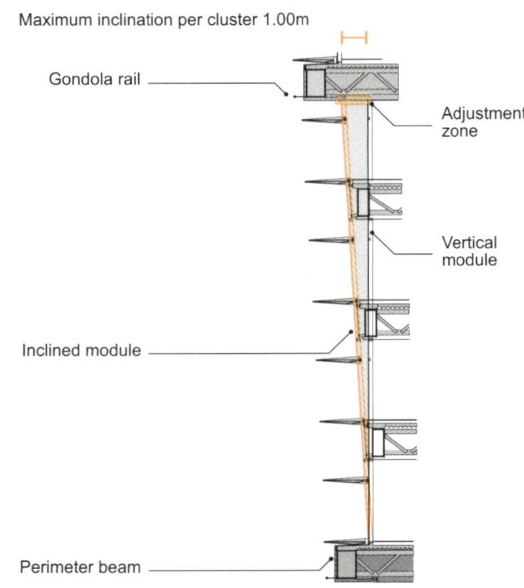

CLUSTER SECTION
FAÇADE OVERHANG

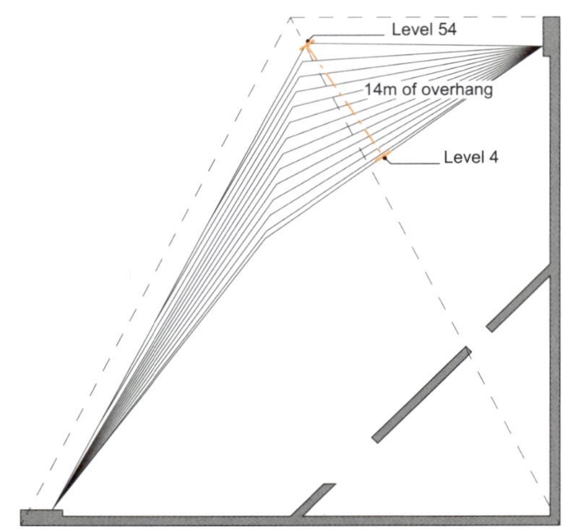

SCHEMATIC SECTION
14.00 m WARP AND OVERHANG

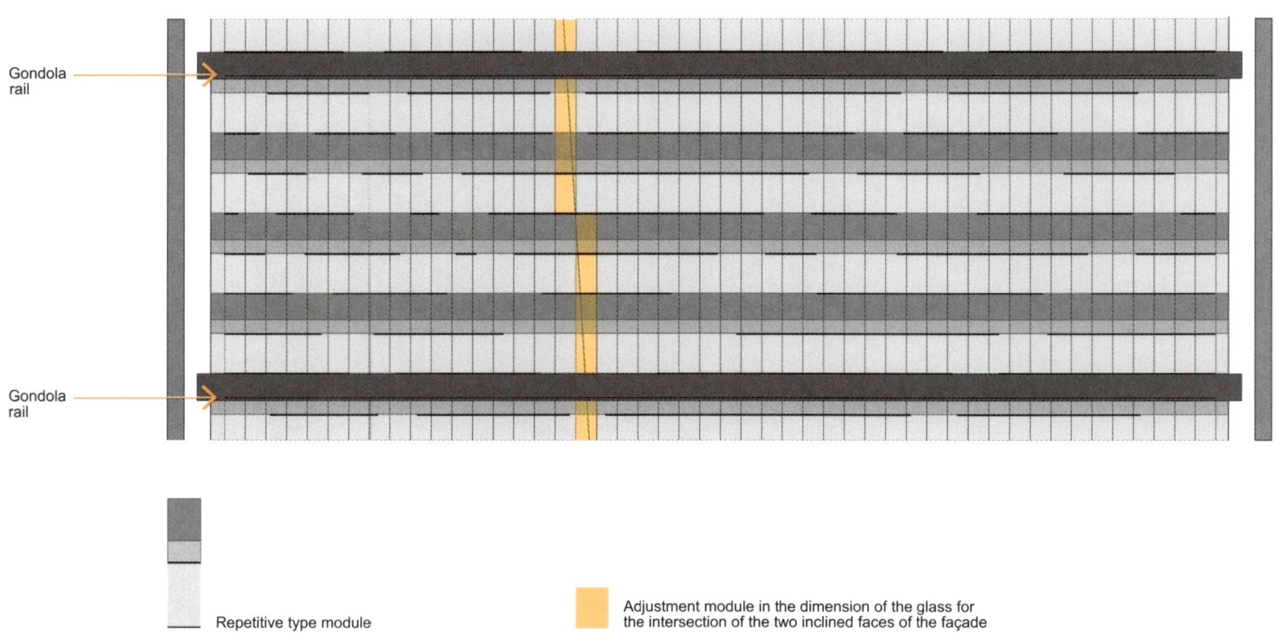

DETAIL LOCATION OF REPEATING MODULES AND ADJUSTMENT MODULES

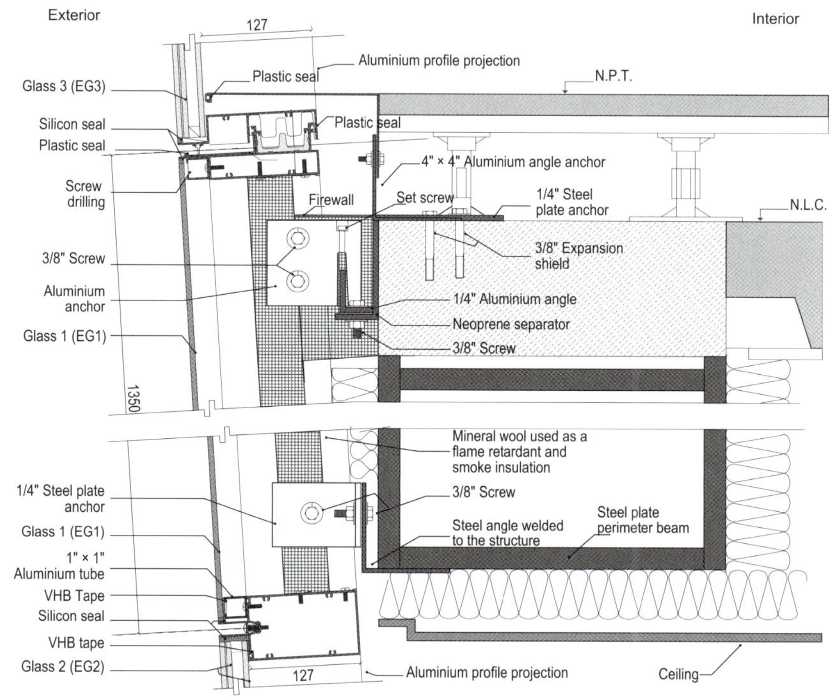

DETAIL 01
SECTION OF ALUMINUM ASSEMBLY DESIGNED TO ACHIEVE ADEQUATE SEALING

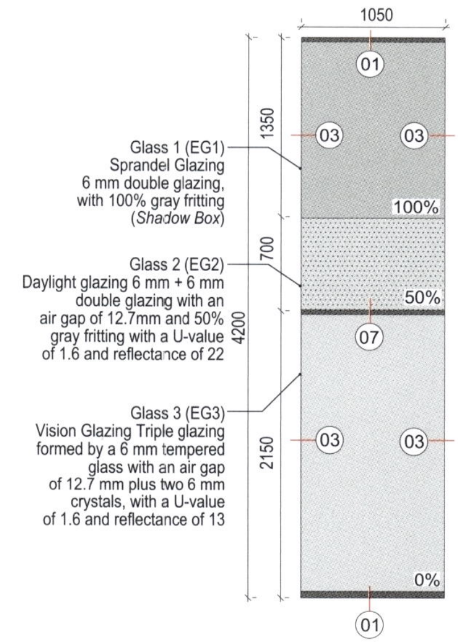

STANDARD REPEATING MODULE

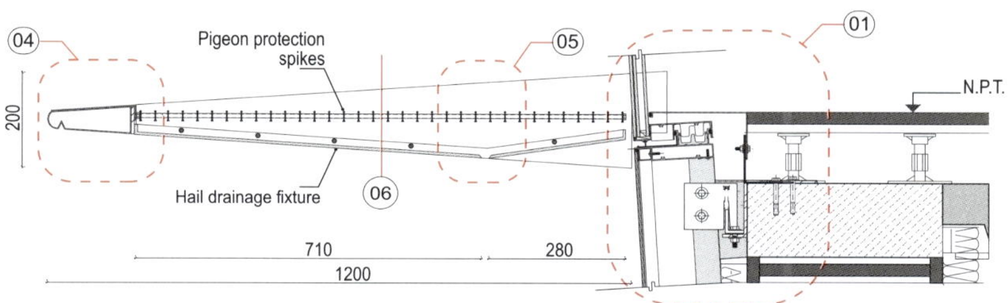

DETAIL 02
STANDARD DETAIL FAÇADE AND MULLION

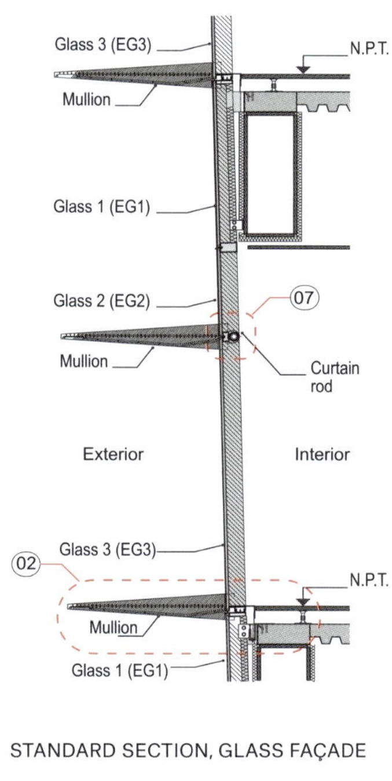

STANDARD SECTION, GLASS FAÇADE

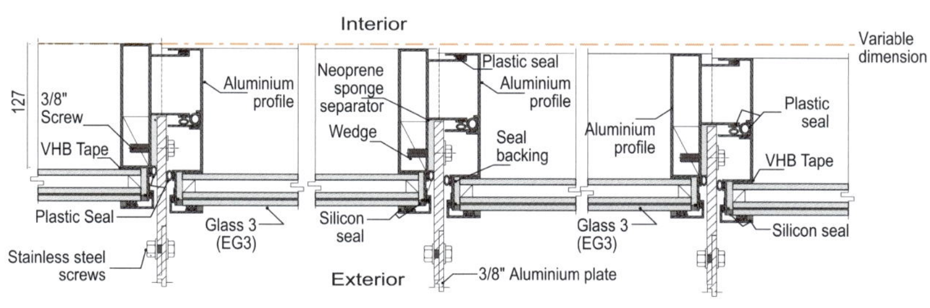

DETAIL 03
PLAN OF ALUMINUM ASSEMBLY DESIGNED TO COMPENSATE FOR WARP

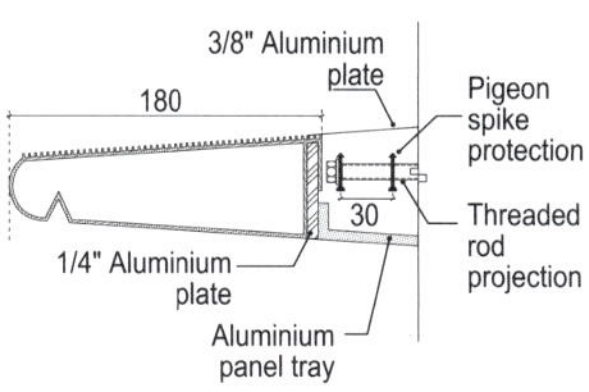

DETAIL 04
MULLION NOSE WITH
ANTI-PIGEON SPIKES

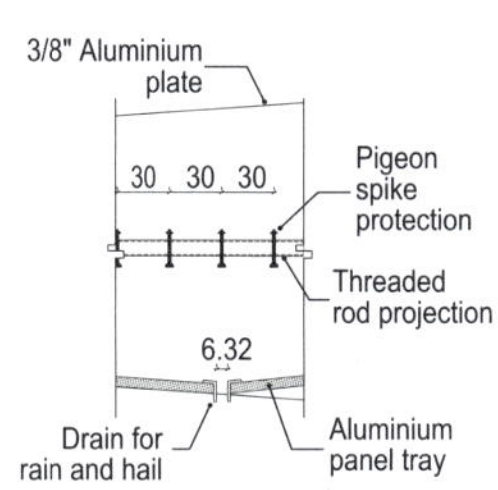

DETAIL 05
MULLION DRAIN WITH
ANTI-PIGEON SPIKES

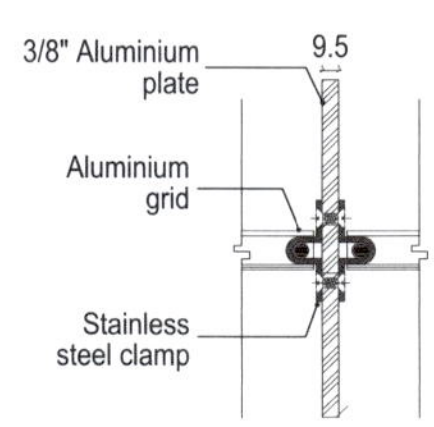

DETAIL 06
STRUCTURAL PLATE
FOR CANTILEVER

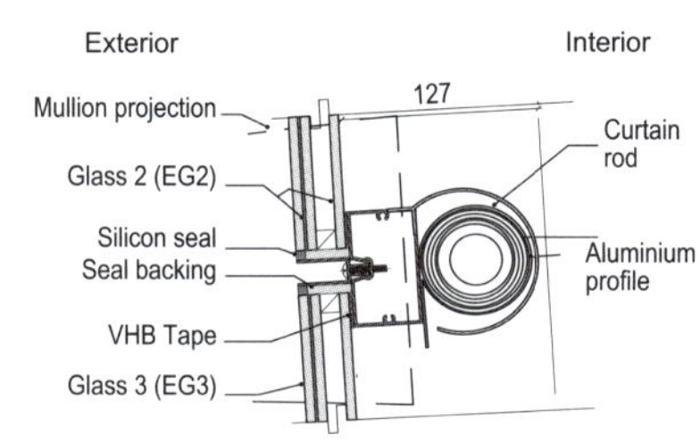

DETAIL 07
SECTION ALUMINUM PROFILE
AND CURTAIN ROD

CONSTRUCTION PROCESS

1–8. Load-bearing test

In order to test the soil's load-bearing capacity, two custom-built piles were load tested to plunging failure and we also performed an analysis of soil mechanics. The pile construction included a metal casing along the sides of the future parking areas in order to improve the accuracy of the soil's load-bearing readings.

9–33. Diaphragm wall

Around the property's perimeter, 60-m deep slurry walls were built as a soil retaining system and as part of the underground construction. These walls also provided the building's foundations. Due to the project's depth, reinforcing cages were spliced together and Soletanche Bachy's technology (13) was used to ensure that water is permanently prevented from filtering into the basement areas. Rebars were left exposed for subsequent connection to the foundation slab's steel reinforcements (under pressure).

2

3

7

8

11

12

13

14

19

20

23

24

25

26

27

28

29

34–91. Moving the house

Using a diamond-cutting disc, we made openings into the original stone foundation in order to pass a rebar cage in two directions. When we poured, the house's original foundations were encased in concrete, providing great stability to the brick and stone house. To transfer the house's load onto the skid-shoes, we inserted steel elements into the waffle slab solid head. We nicknamed them "Cleopatras" due to their resemblance to the litters used to transport Cleopatra in the film. We displaced the house in 11 hours, and returned it to its original location in just 3 hours.

34

37

38

41

42

43

44

48

49

50

30

31

32

33

35

36

39

40

45

46

47

51

52

53

54

55

56

60

To support the new cantilever bearing the weight of the house a reinforcing wall was built, attached to the stone wall with anchoring pins set in staggered rows.

61

66

67

68

72

73

76

77

57

58

59

62

63

64

65

69

70

71

74

The "Cleopatras" rested on the skid shoes, which displaced the concrete tray.

75

78

79

80

81

February 14, the day the house was first displaced.

82

86

87

88

92–102. Ground-level slab

The ground-level slab and the ground-floor assembly are designed to absorb the horizontal pressures exerted on the structure during seismic activity and under the force of wind. Metal tensors and "patas de gallo"—triple-sided, reinforced and embedded elements—were embedded into the concrete slab to transmit the forces from ground-floor structure downward to the foundation walls.

92

95

96

99

100

83

84

85

89

90

91

93

94

97

98

101

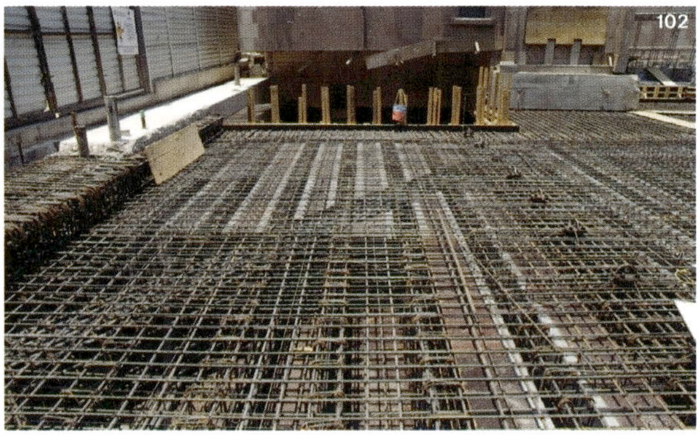
102

103–124. Below-ground levels

The underground levels were built using the top-down system, which uses the project's final slabs as retaining walls. More than 72,000 m³ of soil was excavated to create space for the basement floors to compensate the building's foundation, rendering it unnecessary to include the foundation piles as originally contemplated.

103

106

107

110

111

Like in a history laboratory, the geological strata were visible.

116

117

118

121

Approximately five hours after pouring, areas smaller than 9 m² were cut with a diamond disc to prevent uneven cracks appearing.

122

104

105

108

109

112

113

114

115

119

120

123

124

125–146. Spiral ramp

The property's small footprint, combined with the regulatory requirement for parking facilities, created more than 600 spaces in the building's underground levels. A complex spiral ramp avoids bottlenecks at the entrance and exit; the system includes one permanent ramp for the entrance, another one for the exit, and a third one to enable two-way traffic on a flexible basis during peak hours. The three ramps are spatially interweaved in a spiral of significant design complexity in the design, circulation and construction.

125

128

129

130

134

135

138

139

142

143

144

126

127

131

132

133

136

137

140

141

145

146

147–220. Exposed concrete wall

This is the most important structural element, requiring particular attention to the formwork design, the strategy for pouring the concrete, the removal of the formwork, and the quality of the concrete itself.

147

148

149

153

154

155

156

160

161

165

166

167

The initial chemical process of the concrete creates high temperatures that cause thermal cracks when formwork is removed. Heavy-duty curtains were installed to create a better microclimate, preventing these thermal cracks from appearing.

169

150

151

152

157

158

159

162

163

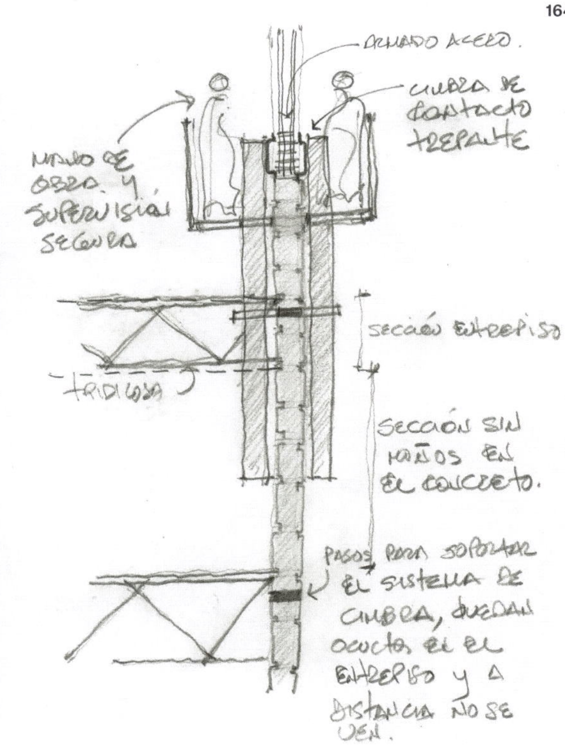

164

168

170

171

172

173

174

The embedded steel connection varies in each cluster, requiring a specific rotation to incorporate the structural axis into the embedded column.

178

182

183

184

185

190

191

192

196

197

198

199

175

176

177

179

180

181

186

187

188

189

193

194

195

200

201

202

203

204

205

209

210

211

212

217

218

219

220

224

225

228

229

206

207

208

213

214

215

216

221–229. Huge X elements were embeded in the concrete wall, to allow the building to bend in seismic and wind events. The natural flexibility of the X elements demanded the insertion of provisional columns to control the adecuated position within the concrete wall.

221

223

226

227

230–232. Self-climbing concrete pump

The concrete pump climbed up along with the formwork. The reach of its telescopic boom was long enough to deliver the concrete efficiently all along the tower's wall and across the floorslabs.

230

231

232

233–241. Crane

A total of three cranes were used for the construction. Given the site's small footprint, their masts needed to be set into the concrete foundations of the building itself. The team's professionalism avoided any electric shock during storms. A significant mechanical manufacturing failure of crane number 3 required the operator to rest the equipment on a neighboring roof, averting a potentially more serious problem.

233

236

237

238

239

242–313. Metal structure

The use of the lightweight yet resistant *tridilosa* steel-and-concrete structure made it possible to span large open distances with a lower density of steel than normally required. The detailed workshop plans, manufacturing quality and assembly of the structure were all crucial in the ability to expose the building's structure as an architectural element. The structural tensioners, gusset plates, metal and *triditrabe* ("pyramid") beams all work harmoniously with the sturdy concrete walls.

242

246

247

248

249

254

255

256

234

235

240

241

243

244

250

251

252

253

257

258

259

260

261

265

268

269

272

273

274

278

279

280

281

262

263

267

270

271

275

276

277

282

283

284

285

286

291

292

295

296

297

302

303

304

305

309

310

287

288

289

290

293
COREY

294

298

299

300

301

306

307

308

311

312

313

314–325. Temporary formwork props

The assembly of the metal structures requires provisional bracing structures, and particularly in the case of mixed structures, these supports need to remain in place until the concrete has been properly cured and becomes stable. The building's architecture required a design of formwork props that could work in cantilever. The topographical record of the bracing's removal was vitally important for the building's final structural appearance.

314

319

320

321

322

326–334. Swimming pool

The swimming pool´s construction was designed to be congruent with the corresponding structural process. We paid particular care in our use of materials and the soldering of the exposed metal structure in order to ensure the required water tightness, aesthetic appearance, and hygiene. Sadly, the tenant decided to line the swimming pool with mosaic tiles, turning it into a regular swimming pool.

326

329

330

335–351. Structural connections

The connections' original design was altered to fit in with the building's architectural image, as well as to ensure the construction is efficient and complies with structural regulations.

335

315

316

317

318

323

324

325

327

328

331

332

333

334

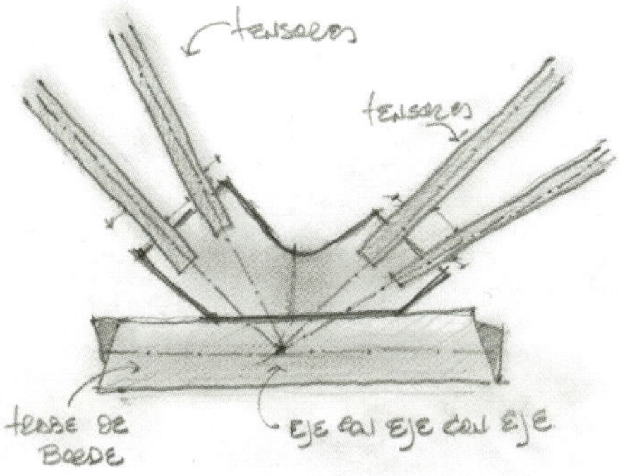

336

337

338

339

340

341

345

346

347

352–364. Staircases

The metal staircases were designed to be used after the construction process; at the end of the construction process they were all cleaned up and painted. We decided to make them work as cantilevers to counter the verticality allowance that naturally happens during the construction process. The stairs are supported by a voided structure with pressurized ductwork for emergency egress in the event of a fire.

352

353

357

358

359

365–398. Auditorium

The tensional structure of the auditorium allows a feeling of levitation, resulting from a difficult assembly process and the use of complex provisional props.

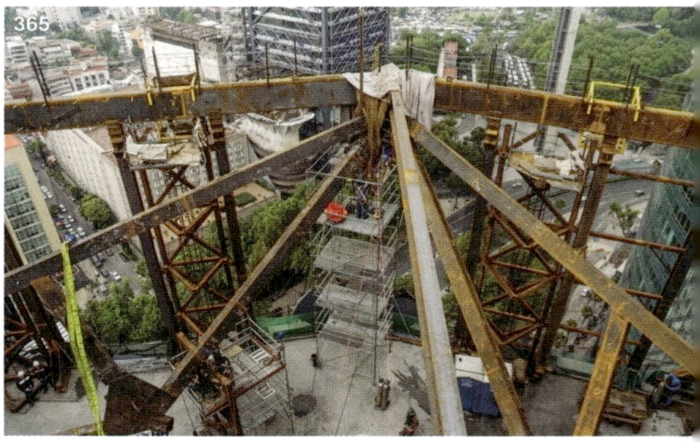
365

342

343

344

348

349

350

351

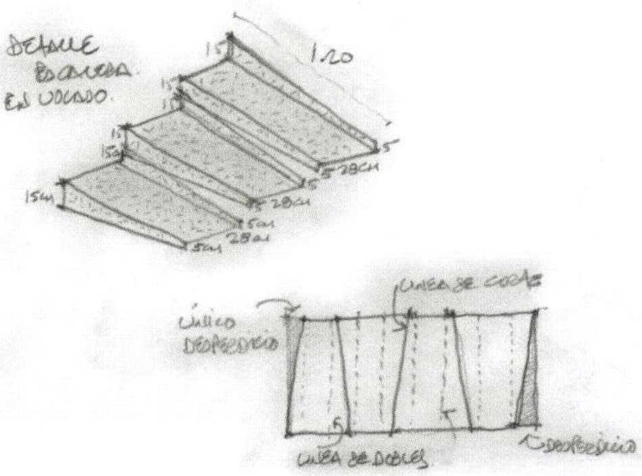
354

355

356

360

361

362

363

364

366

367

368

369

372

373

376

377

378

381

382

387

388

389

370

371

374

375

379

380

383

384

385

386

390

391

392

393

394

395

399–407. Girdles

Four girdles transfer the load of the robotic parking building to the concrete walls, freeing up the building's ground floor and underground levels from the need for bulky columns while also ensuring the building has an essential spatial flexibility in its use.

399

403

404

405

408–445. Robotic parking facility

The robotic parking facility is designed to be eventually recycled as a livable space, when parking space regulations and urban habits move away from the use of cars.

408

409

413

414

415

396

397

398

400

401

402

06

407

410

411

412

416

417

418

419

420

424

425

429

430

431

432

438

439

440

441

446–469.
Shuttle building

Express elevators, electrical transformers substations, chilled water pumps, drinking and fire reservoir water tanks, pumps and emergency egress stairs flow harmoniously through this building.

446

447

448

421

422

423

426

427

428

433

434

435

436

437

442

443

444

445

451

452

453

454

458

459

460

464

465

466

470–509. Sloping structure

The façade's sloping structure is prone to suffer from solar gain and water leaking. The design of the sloped façade system solves these potential problems by using naturally-ventilated layers. The first exposed layer is made of glass fiber reinforced concrete (GFRC), supported by an independent galvanized structure. The second layer consists of metal insulating panels, which regulate the interior temperature, providing water sealing and routing possible water leaks toward the lower apex where it can be collected. This façade design is also protected by a third layer composed of fire-retardant drywall panels.

470

474

475

455

456

457

461

462

463

467

468

469

471

472

473

476

477

478

479

480

481

482

487

488

493

494

495

500

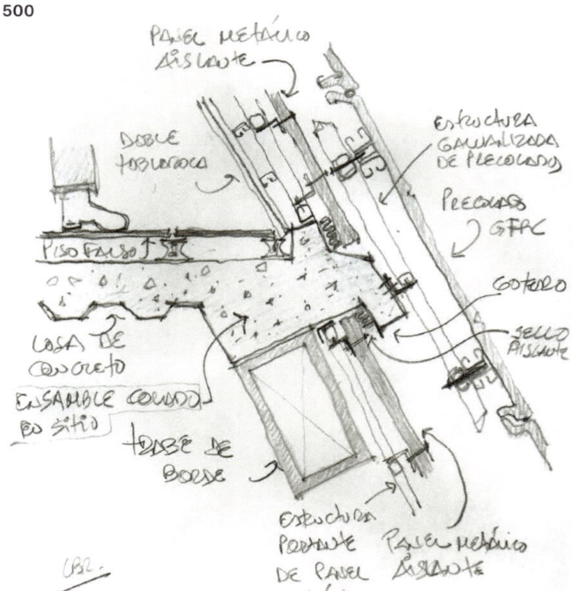

501

505

506

483

484

485

486

489

490

491

492

496

497

498

499

502

503

504

507

508

509

510–534. Ground-floor assembly

ARUP's design for the ground-floor assembly is exclusively in response to the building's structural needs to withstand the forces of the wind and earthquakes. The assembly's hinges with the metal beams embedded in the ground-floor slab exist to ensure the building's stability. We decided to leave this permanently exposed due to its structural attractiveness and because it indicates how the building's structure works.

510

514

515

516

520

521

522

525

526

530

531

511

512

513

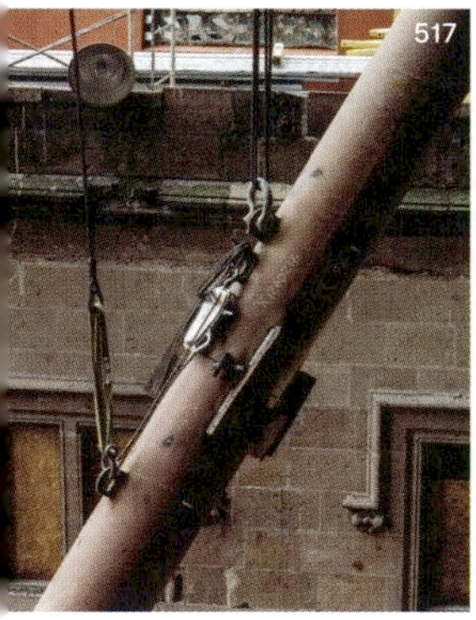
517

518

519

523

524

527

528

529

532

533

53

535–556. Ground-floor lobby (glass box)

The relationship between the early-20th century mansion and the modern high-rise building required a transparent architectural solution. In memory of the demolished courtyard, we proposed the use of a glass ceiling supported by V-shaped reinforcements, and we pulled back the two glass façades in order to leave the house's original stonework untouched.

535

538

539

540

541

545

546

547

551

552

553

557–593. Glass façade structure

The curvature of the glazed façade, as well as our intention to use standard-sized modules, led to the design of identical 2.1 by 1.05 m pieces, which combine to create the curved surface. The modules used to produce the façade's central apex are the only ones made to measure.

557

536

537

542

543

544

548

549

550

554

555

556

558

559

560

561

562

563

566

567

568

573

574

575

576

579

580

581

587

588

589

564

565

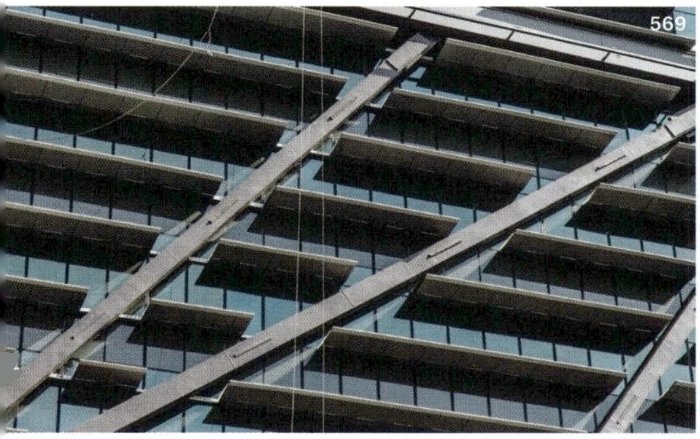
569

570

571

572

577

578

582

583

584

585

586

590

591

592

593

594–639. MEP installations

Temperature control systems (594–601), nocturnal extraction (602), electrical (603–608), hydrosanitary (609–610), fire protection (611–612), water treatment (613), voice and data (614), and elevators (615). Of note is the spatial efficiency demanded by the building installations. Traditionally, buildings use a lot more space for machine rooms and ducts than was achieved here.

594

597

598

599

603

604

607

608

611

612

613

614

595

596

600

601

602

605

606

609

610

615

616

617

618

619

620

624

625

628

629

630

631

632

635

636

640–643. Gondola

The sloping glazed façade (14 meters out of plumb) required a specially-designed gondola to take the cantilever. Like the building itself, 14 rails were designed (matching the number of clusters) to transport the gondola horizontally and to minimize the overhang effect generated by the building's cantilever.

640

621

622

623

626

627

633

634

637

638

639

641

642

643

644–668. Finishes

The finishes in the lobbies and restrooms are designed with allowances and openings in order to absorb seismic movements. The marble paving stones are supported by stainless steel metal fixtures that allow them to absorb the effects of seismic and wind forces. Concrete curbs as well as fire-retardant and waterproof walls were used to ensure the quality of the building's performance and impermeability. Materials were chosen on the basis of their longevity and the LEED requirements for using materials sourced from a maximum of 500 miles from the site.

647

648

649

653

654

657

658

659

662

663

664

644

645

646

650

651

652

655

656

660

661

665

666

667

668

COMPLETED PROJECT

BBVA Bancomer

BBVA Bancomer
ST REGIS
MAPF

BBVA Bancomer

Selecciones

5520 0027

TU DOMINO'S
RECIÉN HORNEADA
PEPPERONI O QUESO
ORIGINAL MEDIANA, EN MOSTRADOR
$85
NADIE
LO HACE
COMO
DOMINO'S

PARQUE LIRA
AV JALISCO
18
40

MacStore

TORRE REFORMA

TORRE REFORMA

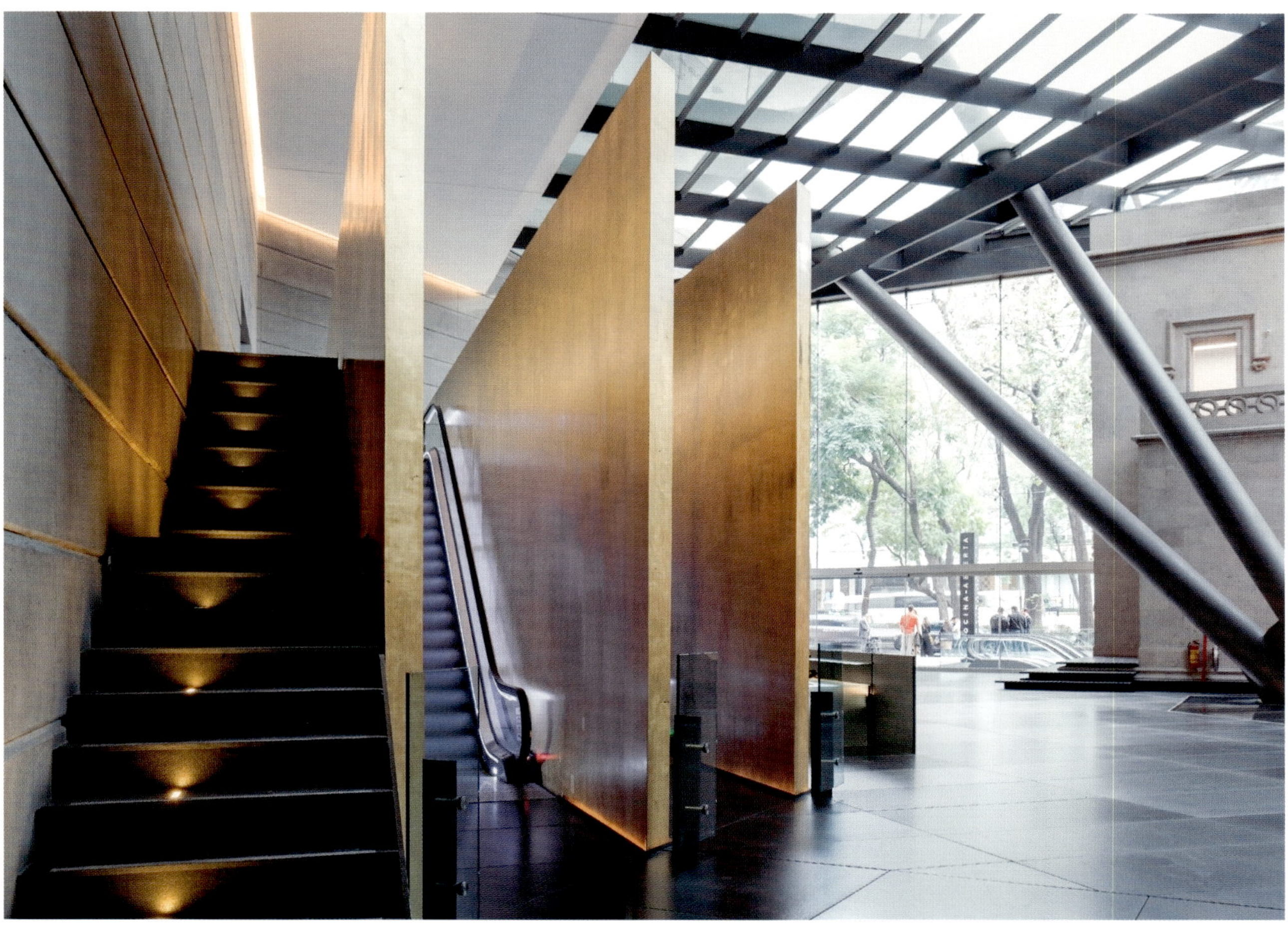

5520 0027

Z
Y
V
U

V
U

TORRE REFORMA

BBVA Bancomer

ANECDOTES

L. BENJAMÍN ROMANO

The project's scope and scale gave rise to all kinds of anecdotes, and we thought it would be interesting to highlight some of them that go beyond the work of architecture itself.

Benjamín Romano: I'd like to begin by talking about the experience with James Bond, it's a great story! One day we received a letter signed by James Bond 007—literally—to ask us for a 3D model of Torre Reforma. We were told that some sequences of a Bond film, *Spectre*, were going to be shot in Mexico City, and the producers were worried that the film would age, before its release, since the tower would only be completed after the film's release. Of course, we shared the 3D model, and if you look carefully at the film, you will notice that when James Bond escapes by flying in a helicopter down Paseo de la Reforma, the tower is complete. We hadn't yet seen in it in context until we went to the movies to see the film. Of course, we had to sign all the relevant legal paperwork.

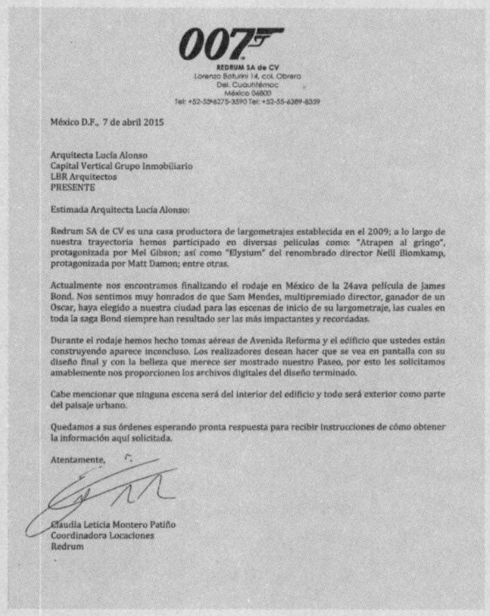

REDRUM SA de CV
Lorenzo Boturini 14, col. Obrera
Del. Cuauhtémoc
México 06800
Tel: +52-55-6275-3590 Tel: +52-55-6389-8359

México D.F., 7 de abril 2015

Arquitecta Lucía Alonso
Capital Vertical Grupo Inmobiliario
LBR Arquitectos
PRESENTE

Estimada Arquitecta Lucía Alonso:

Redrum SA de CV es una casa productora de largometrajes establecida en el 2009; a lo largo de nuestra trayectoria hemos participado en diversas películas como: "Atrapen al gringo", protagonizada por Mel Gibson; así como "Elysium" del renombrado director Neill Blomkamp, protagonizada por Matt Damon; entre otras.

Actualmente nos encontramos finalizando el rodaje en México de la 24ava película de James Bond. Nos sentimos muy honrados de que Sam Mendes, multipremiado director, ganador de un Oscar, haya elegido a nuestra ciudad para las escenas de inicio de su largometraje, las cuales en toda la saga Bond siempre han resultado ser las más impactantes y recordadas.

Durante el rodaje hemos hecho tomas aéreas de Avenida Reforma y el edificio que ustedes están construyendo aparece inconcluso. Los realizadores desean hacer que se vea en pantalla con su diseño final y con la belleza que merece ser mostrado nuestro Paseo, por esto les solicitamos amablemente nos proporcionen los archivos digitales del diseño terminado.

Cabe mencionar que ninguna escena será del interior del edificio y todo será exterior como parte del paisaje urbano.

Quedamos a sus órdenes esperando pronta respuesta para recibir instrucciones de cómo obtener la información aquí solicitada.

Atentamente,

Claudia Leticia Montero Patiño
Coordinadora Locaciones
Redrum

007 letter

On another occasion, the security guards at the building entrance came to look for me, and said: "Sir, there's someone downstairs who says he's called Rafael Moneo, and that you know who he is. He wants to take a look around the building." Of course, I went down immediately to welcome him and introduce myself (I didn't know him personally). He apologized for having turned up out of the blue, and said that he had two spare hours and he was interested in learning more about the building due to its impressive volume. As I went down to meet him, I notified all the architects working with me and summoned them to the meeting room, while I explained the project to him. After we finished, we briefly toured the construction, and after the visit we asked him various questions. His answers were fascinating. He gave us a masterclass on the evolution of urbanism over time; he talked about the importance of the house's coexistence with the tower; he imagined that we hadn't understood him properly, and invited us onto the street to explain his view on the evolution of the Paseo de la Reforma, and said: "Look how this construction coexists with the Social Security building or how the building by Rogers and Legorreta speaks of a different era." He went on to name various buildings explaining to us how they communicated with each other. He placed great emphasis on how the coexistence of constructions from different epochs give the Paseo de la Reforma its interesting character, although he only identified Torre Bancomer and Torre Reforma as modern buildings.

Site visit with Rafael Moneo

Miquel Adrià: Rafael Moneo's perception is key, because he designed the Bankinter building in Madrid, which preserved a small pre-existing mansion on La Castellana, and added a new building at a slight angle behind. He understood your project perfectly because he also faced the same challenge in Madrid. He also loved it, as he remarked to me.

BR: It was a wonderful experience and he congratulated us warmly on the building afterwards.

MA: Tell us about the visit by [Mexico's former president] Ernesto Zedillo.

BR: A former student from the Iboeramericana University came to the work site and also asked to see me. He told me "Benjamín, I've come to see you because my father-in-law wants to come to visit your project." I asked him "Who's your father-in-law?" to which he replied "Ernesto Zedillo". I simply exclaimed "*Órale*! Tell him that he's welcome." And that is the story behind Ernesto Zedillo's visit. I was very impressed by his modesty. When he arrived, we received him in the meeting room. For this visit, I invited my mother, my brothers, and the building's Mexican investors. We had a very interesting chat about what he does in Yale as the director of the Yale Center for the Study of Globalization. He told us how happy he is working there, and that he is depressed by all the security measures needed in Mexico, because in Yale it's completely different. He said to us: "I can walk alone from my house, queue up like everyone else for my coffee, and for me that's a better kind of life."

MA: What observations did he make? He has two sons who are architects and so I imagine he understands architecture.

BR: He stressed the importance of preserving the pre-existing house; he mentioned that during his administration he would like to have done the same with the Social Security building which is located on Paseo de la Reforma. In fact, he recommended that I should try to buy the building in order to reuse it; I did try and was promptly rebuffed. He also queried why the building had its back turned away from the Angel of Independence monument, because that was something that disconcerted him. I explained to him that it was a difficult decision for me, due to the architectural scheme, the views over Chapultepec Park, the fact that our façade looking toward the monument is an adjacency, and other issues. He clearly understood but repeated: "you turned your back on the Angel of Independence; see how all of the monuments on Paseo de la Reforma face east because that is the direction of the seat of government and therefore it's an act of respect for the country's institutions." This comment revealed to me that his political beliefs eclipsed his architectural vision. But the rest of the visit was very positive, relaxed and interesting, both for us and all of the workers on the site who came up to greet him. Then came the visit of Teodoro González de León, who later sent me a card which is now one of my cherished possessions. When Teodoro came to see the building, he described it as Piranesi-like, due to the complexity he saw in the construction process; remember that during the construction we were using some very sturdy props, and when they were removed they left the space completely unobstructed. In the building's core there were some recently mounted beams and evacuation stairs everywhere. Just at the time of Teodoro's visit, the auditorium was a structure held up by props; he saw everything in its exposed state, and I imagine the chaotic appearance led him to comment: "this is like a construction devised by Piranesi." Another strong memory is that I said that I wasn't going to use any finish on the foundation walls

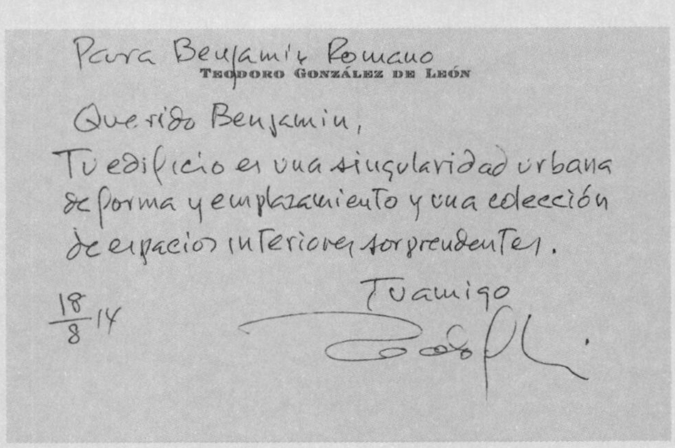

Para Benjamín Romano
TEODORO GONZÁLEZ DE LEÓN
Querido Benjamín,
Tu edificio es una singularidad urbana de forma y emplazamiento y una colección de espacios interiores sorprendentes.
18/8/14
Tu amigo

Site visit with Teodoro González de León, image of core under construction. Note from Teodoro González de León.

Marriage proposal

Photography: Ernesto Rivas

Alexander Schultz, walking on a tightrope from Torre Bancomer to Torre Reforma to break the world record.

—the diaphragm walls—and that I was going to leave them exposed; he became excited and told me: "that's the brutalism that has sadly been discarded of late. It's wonderful that you're going to leave them like that!" I told this to some of the investors and they said: "Ignore him. Cover them up and give them a coat of paint, they'll definitely look better with a finish."

In the end, I left them exposed.

Undoubtedly Teodoro's most beautiful comment was the one we received the day following his visit, in a card signed by him. The card says that it seemed like a project with surprising spaces, but the best thing about the building was how it was sited on its plot.

MA: And then you had all sorts of other experiences too?
BR: That's right, we had all kinds of thing happening, even a marriage proposal. I love this story: a young man approached us and requested permission to enter the building during the construction process. We asked him what for, and he said that he wanted to get married and that his girlfriend worked in the adjacent Torre Mayor. So he asked me permission to take a large sign up to the equivalent floor where his girlfriend worked; once in position, he telephoned his girlfriend and told her "quick, look out of your window and see what's happening." The girlfriend looked across and saw him holding the little engagement ring box and the sign asking for her to marry him. I know it sounds a little cheesy, but I like that anecdote and it I think it was a very sweet gesture.

MA: And what about the acrobat?
BR: One day, the German acrobat Alexander Schultz turned up to say that he wanted to cross from Torre Bancomer to Torre Reforma on a slack line, in an attempt to break the world record. We thought it sounded interesting and would give him permission provided he secured all the necessary permits—which he did, with authorizations given by the Mexico City government, including from the Ministry of Civil Protection—and the crossing was initially scheduled for October 2. With everything in place, the attempt had to be called off one day before because the weather forecast predicted strong winds which would make the crossing very dangerous. About three months later, he returned with the updated authorizations and this time he succeeded, crossing at a height of 217 meters and breaking a new Urban Highline record.

Another episode involved a site worker who got kicks from throwing objects and trying to hit pedestrians below. Fortunately he always missed, but I felt we were dealing with a potential serial killer. Pablo Duro, the building's project manager, detected the problem and told me: "Benjamín, this isn't an accident. Perhaps if one stone were to fall it might be, although still unlikely due to the protections and protection barriers we have set up, but that many? I think that we've got ourselves a problem here."
MA: How did you find out? Did pedestrians complain, or how else did you become aware of the problem?

Security camera notice

Deformation of one of the cages for the diaphragm wall

BR: Yes, pedestrians were nearly hit by the projectiles—because that's what they become after picking up so much speed—and logically they came to complain. When you're involved in a construction, you receive complaints about everything; people with a broken windscreen will come and say that it was caused by the construction; if cracks appear in the wall of their house, they blame it on the construction, and so on. People will complain about everything, and although some third-party insurance policies do exist, they don't cover this kind of accident, because the insurance's deductible is set so high. In my experience, this happens with every project, and particularly with large-scale ones.

Pablo Duro decided to position undercover police officers on each floor. It seemed to me an expensive and inefficient solution, because the killer would surely notice them and conceal his intentions. We spoke to my nephew Daniel, an expert in security issues, and he recommended installing high-definition cameras on Torre Bancomer, focused on our building. We called the Torre Bancomer people—with whom we were always on good terms—to tell them about our problem and they gave us permission to install the cameras. As part of the strategy, we photographed Pablo Duro from the Torre Bancomer and placed the photographs on the construction site elevators and at the entrance to every level, to intimidate the guilty party. The caption on the photos read: "We're recording you. We'll catch you next time you throw something." He must have left the construction site, because these incidents stopped happening after we stuck up the photographs.

MA: What else happened during the construction process?
BR: Another experience was the deformation of one of the reinforcing cages used in the diaphragm wall, beside the house's façade. As a safety measure, a double cable is always used during the entire lifting process, and on this occasion there was an accident which caused the main cable to break. When this lifting cable broke, the backup cable took the weight of the cage. In the end nothing serious happened, but logically the cage became deformed. During a normal operation of sinking the rebar cage into the wall, this would not have even been an issue, but the tricky aspect in this case was that we were placing it in the walls that surround the house, which were placed 20 cm from the listed façade. As you know, the walls are 60 m deep and the cages are inserted into the ground in two sections, each measuring 30 m (plus overlaps). When we were maneuvering it, one of the cables broke and the 20 cm separation was not enough to accommodate the cage's deformation. Fortunately, the deformation bulged away from the façade rather than facing toward it, thus preventing any damage to the stonework. It was a tense moment, but the safety systems were adequate and the maneuvering could be completed without causing any harm to the listed house's façade.

We also had the widely reported case of the crane resting on the rooftop of the Torre Mayor. I remember being in the local government offices doing some administrative paperwork, when Pablo Duro called to tell me what had happened, confirming that no one was injured and that

The crane resting on the roof of Torre Mayor

the damage only amounted to a few broken paving slabs on the roof of the Torre Mayor's lower volume. I visited the site and was shocked to find the press filming and taking photographs of the scene. I wanted to climb up to the rooftop to see the damage for myself when I found that I was not allowed into the Torre Mayor. The following day I discovered that Felipe Flores—the administrator of Torre Mayor—had sued me for the damages caused to Torre Mayor's rooftop. As I expected, the lawsuit was dismissed because I wasn't even the one responsible for the accident, and in any case only minor damages were caused. In the event, we didn't even meet the amount of the insurance deductible. A manufacturing defect had caused a part of the crane to break, and the operator decided to rest it on the Torre Mayor's rooftop in order to prevent the crane's possible collapse and possible fatal consequences. In my view, the operator made the right decision, although the people at the Torre Mayor over-reacted with the media and in the law courts, closing down our construction site for a month. Gonzalo Robina—a director of Fibra Uno—eventually had to act as a go-between in order to improve our neighborly relations with the Torre Mayor.

There's another anecdote I like. The house was moved on Saturday, February 14. At the end of the day, I left the site exhausted by the stress of the operation. As you can imagine, I looked terrible. At 11 pm I went home to rest, and I was stopped by police who were doing breathalyzer tests and the officers, seeing that I looked worse for wear, were suspicious and stopped me. Of course, I hadn't drunk anything, but they refused to let me continue on my way until I had passed the test. Early the following morning, after a few short rest, I received a call from a friend complaining to me that the feat of moving the house had lost him a lot of money because he had placed a bet that during the process of moving the house I would cause it to collapse and simply say sorry and then build the tower without anything to worry about. After I hung up the telephone, I admit that I was experiencing stress as never before, because I realized that if the building had accidentally fallen down, it would have affected many people, including those at the National Institute of Fine Arts, the city government, Doctor Roberto Meli, the investors, the project itself and my architecture firm. Clearly the adrenaline of the design process and the preparation for the house's movement never allowed me to consider the possibility that something might go wrong, but when I received that call my stress level hit the roof. It felt like a bad hangover. At that moment I said to Rosi, my wife: "Let's go to the site and see how the house spent the night," she told me that she couldn't because she was looking after our grandson José; I asked her to bring him with us and so we went to the site. When Rosi was walking with our grandson on the pavement of Paseo de la Reforma, she heard an argument between a pair of cyclists. The woman was saying to her partner: "I promise you, yesterday the house was here!" He answered: "You're crazy, a house can't just have moved in one night." Then Rosi intervened and told them: "In fact, sir, the house *did* use to be here, and yesterday they moved it 18 meters."

MA: After the call and time for reflection, would you do the same again?

BR: Definitely, but I would involve everyone else in the risk. I don't know if I'm explaining myself, but I told everyone: "It's not going to fall down... I'm sure that we can move it without any trouble." Everyone believed in me, and although I think that they imagined some kind of risk, they always saw that I was very confident that the famous concrete "tray" would work and the house wouldn't fall down. I'm one hundred per cent sure that I'd do the same again, but I would share the risk and stress because I absorbed it all myself and I'm sure it has taken years off my life.

MA: And the financing, how did that work out?
BR: I often accompanied the partners to explain the project and proudly told them that we would be making the tallest building in the city, that we were in the middle of the process of moving a stone-and-mortar construction, that the building wouldn't have foundation piles nor any interior columns; of course, we also talked about the smaller construction budget. I remember seeing how many financiers just stared at me without saying a word, and I suppose that after we were leaving the meeting room they all collapsed in laughter, because I'm sure that everything I said sounded like a pipedream, and people in finance are risk averse. One day one of the partners told me: "stop saying that the building doesn't have columns, because no one believes you." I remember answering: "What do you want me to do, pencil in some columns on the plans?" He just told me to stop saying it.

After successfully moving the house, and building up confidence through Arup, the credit was made available. This anecdote strikes me as interesting because it's very difficult to head into uncharted waters, and when you propose new ideas, people simply don't want to take the risk.

In the end, the tower was built without columns and without foundation piles; we moved the house, and the total cost of the project was only 12% above our original estimate. But breaking the financial ice in the face of the unknown is an uphill struggle and requires a lot of daring.

MA: How did Arup end up using the *tridilosa* pyramid slabs in their structural design?
BR: When Heberto Castillo died, Federico Alcaraz had finished writing and editing the second and third volumes of *Análisis y diseño de estructuras* which Heberto had begun. When I decided to work with Arup, I explained to them my plan to use the *tridilosa* pyramid slabs, and I went to New York with a copy of Heberto's books and with the engineer Alcaraz to help me explain how *tridilosa* worked. We held meetings with various Arup engineers, presided over by David Scott, and Alcaraz explained how this design worked structurally. Scott asked him if there was an English version of the books, and I remember Alcaraz told him: "no, there isn't one, but that's not a problem at all, we can get them translated." Afterwards he asked for bibliographical references on the issue and he answered: "I'm the only

Tridilosa pyramid slabs

living bibliography, because Heberto is no longer with us and I'm the one who recorded Heberto's ideas in the text." This comment saddened me greatly because it's a shame that Heberto's theories only live on in the minds of a handful of people, and I think that these great ideas should have reached a wider audience. In the end, Arup translated the books and the entire building was designed with *triditrabes*, which they dubbed "Pyramid Beams." The benefits of these pyramid beams can be elucidated with an anecdote about Corey, the company that handled the building's metal structure. When Corey received the invitation to enter a bid for the structural component, they assumed that we had made a major miscalculation in the volume of steel required, and just like the financiers, they wrote us off as amateurs. Therefore, the company decided to enter with a very attractive offer because they imagined that later would come the time for the classic "adjustments" and they would end up compensating for their low offer. At the end of the construction, Corey's CEO, Rene Calderón, told me: "we sold you pure air and not only that, we had to transport it into Mexico City." As you know, the *tridilosa* pyramid beams use the height of their span (or air) to give them inertia.
MA: So in fact, instead of selling you air, they sold you the true weight of the steel and that's why their numbers didn't work out well for them.

BR: That's right, because there was a large volume but little steel. We had a similar experience with Vinci Constructions, Europe's largest construction company. It's a French firm with lots of divisions, one of them being Soletanche Bachy, the parent company of Cimesa in Mexico.

At the invitation of Pierre Guiot—Cimesa's CEO—I travelled to Paris and they said that they were very interested in participating in the building's construction and submitting a quote for it. So we requested their quote, and I suppose that they simply multiplied the number of square meters by what it generally costs to build a similar construction in Europe, and their final figure was far higher than the amount for which we had budgeted. When we received the quote, everyone started going crazy here because I insisted that the building would cost far less than their estimate, and I told them that the French had surely got their numbers wrong. Thanks to Pierre's influence, they sent over a Peruvian engineer to work with Julieta to produce a better quote and they did a good job. Another issue we had with them was Vinci's insistence on pouring concrete for the walls in sections 2.4 m high instead of 70 cm high (which is how we built it), arguing that this would make the construction process more efficient.

Perhaps these anecdotes make me come across as being overly arrogant.

MA: Rather than arrogant, I'd say enthusiastic, or naïve.

BR: "Naïve" might well be the right word, but let me explain why I said arrogant. Imagine the scene when I told the director of Vinci that they did not know how to quantify, or when we were arguing about the height of the concrete pours for the wall, and with him considering that my suggestion was less efficient than his one. To me it seems a little bit like what we were talking about earlier with the bankers: when you propose something different, you're simply taking them out of their comfort zone.

MA: Something like David and Goliath.

BR: Perhaps, but I don't think it's about strength. I think that it's a matter of knowing and understanding your proposal. Remember when Buckminster Fuller asked Norman Foster: "How much does your building weigh, Mr. Foster?..." In my opinion it's exactly the same situation, when an architect understands his design, it is easier to persuade others about different ideas.

Working session with Selene Patlán and Miquel Adrià

Night of the final concrete wall pouring

APPENDIX

TORRE REFORMA

TORRE REFORMA

TORRE REFORMA CREDITS BY COMPANY

LBR&A-Diseño
Antonella Morritu
César Balmes
Daniel Vega
Diego Leal
Erick Islas
Gerardo Galicia
Guillermo Arriola
Harón Kababie
Ilan Kellersztain
Jesús Hidalgo
José Luis Martin
Julieta Boy
Kenji Fuentes
Lilian Levy
Lucía Alonso
Mariana Mercado
Mario Salim
Mateo Riestra
Octavio Aguilar
Rafael Arce
Walter Lingard
Zuany Díaz

Fondo Hexa
Agustín Prendes
Alberto Romano
Beatriz Hernandez
Bernardo Calderón
Cristina Almazán
Diana Moreno
Félix Romano
Fredel Romano
Jacobo M. Romano
Jovita Pelcastre
Juan Sánchez
Luis Alvarez
Marco Agustín
Moisés Romano

LBR&A-Construcción
Aladar Razo
Daniel Ocampo
Edmundo Bernal
Flavio Soria
Guadalupe Vega
Guillermo Ramirez
Leoncio Hernandez
Mario Martínez
Mauricio Sánchez
Miguel Rodríguez
Miriam Barajas
Octavio González
Oliver Rodriguez
Olivia Elizalde
Raúl León
Sergio Juárez
Stella Bauleo
Tonatiuh Nava

Arup NY
Adam Pearce
Adrián Pena-Iguaran
Alex Smith
Barnali Ghosh
Bruno Silva
Carlos Molina Hutt
Damian Grant
Daniel Wilcoxon
David Easter
David Scott
Ioannis Kourakis
Jeremy Macht
Judy Coleman-Graves
Karine Charlebois
Kevin Snagg
Marcus Shuttle
Mark Mathey
Matthew Lacey
Nikolas Rodriguez
Ricardo Pittela
Robert Talby
Sanya Levi
Scott Bondi
Tabitha Tavolaro
Zygi Lubkowski

Arup LA
Anait Manjikian
Brian McLaughlin
Bruce McKinlay
Jamey Lyzun
Karen Mozes
Martin Howell
Matt Williams
Michael Hass
Michelle Torres
Nate Wittasek
Nick Antonio
Sara Wood
Tony Freitas
Tony Panossian
Vahan Margaryan
Roberto Meli Piralla

DITEC
Alfredo Hernandez
Armando Mérida
David Contreras
Edgar Lopez
Edgar Pérez
Fernando Alvarez
Héctor Morales
José Alejandro
José Luis Aguilar
Rodolfo Valles
Sergio Valdés

VAMISA
Ismael Vázquez

WSP Kantor Seinuk
Ahmad Rahimian
Bart Sullivan

Mueser Rutledge Consulting Engineers
Raymond Poletto

Soil mechanics
CDMX TGC
Elvira León
Enrique Santoyo†
Erika Valle
José Antonio Segovia†

Bovis
Luis Manuel Sanchez
Matt Ruíz
Pablo Duro
Raúl Berarducci
Raúl Mireles

CIMESA
Adrián Ramirez
Alfredo Cirión
Axel Ramírez
Daniel García
Guy Tillate
Israel Amezquita
Juan Paulín
Julio Alejandrez
Marco Fontana
Miguel Bravo
Miguel Rojas
Octavio Camarena
Olivier Toulemont
Paulina Giles
Pierre Guiot
Rubén Parilli

COREY
Alberto Avelar
Carlos Gerardo Rodríguez
Crispín Quesadas
Gerardo Mendoza
Gustavo Cárdenas
Herminio Soto
Irma Villa
Javier Salas
Javier Villa
Jessica Castillo
Jorge Marín
José Carlos Hernandez
Martín Hernández
Rene Calderón Bujdud
Ricardo Silva
Victor Castillo

Hasset Engineering, Inc.
Patrick Hasset
Tina Xie

RECAL
Enrique Jiménez
Josué Mercado
Rene Calderón Martínez
Ricardo Rodríguez

LOMCCI
Adrián Ramirez
Alejandro Nájera
Asunción Rojo
Crescencio Serna
Eduardo Rodríguez
Francisco Escorza
Jesús Peña
Jorge Velázquez
José Delgado
Juventino Rodriguez
Oscar Gómez
Raymundo Lombera

Promotora de Resistencia
Alberto Barbosa
Israel Amezquita
Marcos García
Sergio Mesa

EFCO
Alfonso Díaz
Andrew Gray
Antonio Dieck
David Whipple
Francisco Islas
Isidro Odena
Julián García
Mauricio Arbelaez
Mike Rasmunssen

ENTEC
Arturo García
Pedro Hernandez
Ruth Lizardi

HEG
Christian Lopez
Fernando Hernandez
Jorge Arizpe
Rafael Claudies
Raymundo Sandoval
Yazmín Lozano

CEMEX
Alberto Rodríguez
Carlos Thomae
Enrique Juárez
Hugo Guerrero
Humberto Domínguez
Javier De la Garza
Kenji Kono
Miguel Garza Zambrano
Sandra Delgado
Silvia Angélica Díaz de León

PRETECSA
Alejandro Fastag
Bernardo Johannsen
Fernando Alcántara
Fidel López
Hugo Enciso

Cívita
Alejandro Bátiz
Dinah Cuevas
Jaime Talavera
Jorge López
Monica Chávez
Paulina Melgoza
Sofía Ruíz

AREI
Darío Ibargüengoitia

Luz + Forma
Jesús Hernández
Luis Lozoya

Van Deusen & Associates
Ahmet Tanyeri
Michael Muñoz

Schindler
Alberto Peralta
Andrea Navarrete
Anthony Turner
Chris Allen
Ignacio Chavero
Isaac Benitez
Knut Ulrich

DYPRO/CYVSA
Alejandro Armella
Carlos Méndez
Isaac Marina
Jonathan Corona
Luis Xavier López
Marta Lopez
Rodrigo Vázquez
Sergio Armella
Victor Argüello
Víctor Armella

Uribe Ingenieros
Alfredo García
Arturo Martínez
César Elizalde
Eduardo Deciga
Erick Brito
Felipe Santos
German Hernández
Guadalupe Gómez
Luis Alberto Patiño
Mijaíl Rodríguez
Raul Uribe

Garza Maldonado & Asociados
Francisco Garza
Salvador padilla

Honeywell
Christian Pereyra
Darío Salto
David García
Eduardo Soto
Gilberto Chávez
Guadalupe Luis
Ivan Salgado
José Luis Cantero
José Luis Zambrano

Aldesa
Blanca Rivas
Caleb Treviño
Ignacio Ayuso
Jorge Teruel
Juan González
Manuel Carpinteyro
Modesto Martínez
Sergio Porras
Ulises González

WÖHR
Eckerhard Stockenberg
Frank Stockenberg
Guillermo de Hoyos
Javier Lachica
Jens Niepelt

Soluciones en piedra Franco
Alejandro Aguilar
Andrés Castro
Elmer Sánchez
Emmanuel Herrera
Ernesto Franco
José Romero
María Luisa Corona
Víctor Ramirez

DEKMAR
Abraham Levy Cherem
Claudio Torres
Elías Levy Cherem
Fernando García
José Medina
Ramón García
Vicente García

NAAGARIA
César Barranco
Jorge Goldberg

Carpenter
Enrique Rivera

Glass
César Aguirre

Layher
Álvaro Guerra
Antonio Dieck

Acabados de calidad
Alejandro Valencia
José Miguel Rodríguez
Lourdes Valencia
Manuel Vázquez
Osvaldo Macedas

FCK Estructuras
Armando Castillo
Carlos Moguel
José Luis Baños
Julio César Mendoza
Miguel Ángel Hernandez

AGR
Agustín Escobedo
Jonathan Perez
María José Velazco
Pablo González

Arquimet
Hugo Agraz
Marcelo Bolaños
Trinidad Martínez

STAFF (Cleaning and operations)
Bernabé Piñuela
Irineo and Celso
Leonel "El Chaparrito" Juárez
Maritza Miranda
Ramiro Bautista
Rodolfo "Ventanas" Román

Stonemason
Enrique Sánchez

ODIS ASVERSA
Alfredo Galván
Francisco Hernández
Juan Luis Herrera
Mauricio Cohen
Rafael Pérez

Wind study
Ali Malkawi
University of Pennsylvania

BIOGRAPHICAL NOTE
L. BENJAMÍN ROMANO

As a student at the Universidad Iberoamericana, he joined the studio of the engineer Heberto Castillo, where he performed calculations of structural loads. A year later he was put in charge of the architectural project for an 19,000 m² industrial complex in the State of Hidalgo, under the direction of Castillo. By August 1978, together with his architecture degree, he had completed the first building of his professional career. Taking an interest in the industrialization of housing construction he was hired by a factory in the State of Israel, where he came to understand two things: that his profession would never be that of mass-produced architectural construction and that architectural design should focus on the structure and construction process.

In 1982, he was awarded an honorable mention upon delivering his thesis, and was invited by his supervisors to teach classes at the Universidad Iberoamericana, where he has been professor of the Project and Construction Cycles. He has taught diplomas, participated in the Coordination of the Construction Cycle and in the review of the curriculum of the School of Architecture, UIA Plan. Since 2003, at the invitation of the architect Francisco Serrano, he has coordinated the Blanca Cemex Chair at the same University. His university education, his early understanding of structures and constructive processes, as well as his continued learning of the profession through teaching, are clearly visible in his projects, which have earned him international recognition:

2018
International Highrise Award

2017
Cemex Building Award for Universal Accessibility

2016–2017
Invited as Expert in Residence by Harvard University

2016
Gold Medal at the 14th Bienal Nacional de Arquitectura Mexicana

Diamond Award, ACEC New York, in Category "C" Structural Systems.

Building of the Year 2016; *Obras* magazine, Grupo Editorial Expansión

2014
Augusto A. Álvarez award for excellence in his architectural career. Federación de Colegio de Arquitecto de México (FCARM)

Silver Medal at the 13th Bienal Nacional de Arquitectura Mexicana, in Category "E" Education

PCI Design Awards Program, Category Education

2012
Silver Medal at the 12th Bienal Nacional de Arquitectura Mexicana, por Innovación Tecnológica, in Category "Restoring Real Estate Patrimony"

2011
Luis Barragán Award for Professional Merit in Professional Architecture Practice; CAM-SAM Awards

2010
Silver Medal at the 11th Bienal Nacional de Arquitectura Mexicana, for the project Torre Tres Picos, in Category "Offices"

1992
First place worldwide for smart buildings, for the IBI building in Chicago, Illinois

TORRE REFORMA was printed in China by Asia Pacific Offset in June 2019. 2,000 copies were printed. The fonts used are from the Atlas family, designed by Susana Carvalho, Kai Bernau and Christian Schwartz and published by Commercial Type in 2012.